WEALTH BUILDING

FOR

BEGINNERS

YOUR MANUAL FOR TAKING CONTROL
OF YOUR FINANCIAL FUTURE, NOW!

By

Edward R. Williams

CONTENTS

FOREWORD

by Stacey Armstrong

I was homeless because of the traumatic experience of losing my job and having no money saved. I relied on a job that I had been working at for 20 years. Before my job termination, I could never imagine my circumstances suddenly changing for the worse, causing me to lose my comfortable lifestyle.

Before my termination, life was great, and I spent money effortlessly. Expensive dining out was a routine along with many other things that contributed to my spending habits. My job paid me a great salary and offered employer benefits, so there was never any sense of urgency to save and invest on my own because I was "fine right now."

My employer was based in Virginia, which is an "at-will employment" state. If you are considered an "at-will" employee, you can be dismissed by an employer for any reason, and without warning, as long as the reason is not illegal. In Virginia, employment relationships are presumed to be "at will," which means that employment term extends for an indefinite period and could be terminated by either party for any reason, or no reason at all, upon reasonable notice.

This happened to me, and it blindsided me, which led me to become homeless after losing my job. I tried re-entering the job market again but experienced major challenges. After having a job that lasted 20 years, my skill set over the years became very job-specific. The fast-paced society we currently live in demands technological and creative intelligence that is tough to learn outside of your prime working years.

Throughout all of this, my faith in God never withered. I trust in God.

One evening our church organized a financial empowerment session and that was when I met Mr. Williams and his team. Edward led a presentation for our church members about the importance of financial planning and his team's signature concept called the Wedge for building an individual's finances. I have sat through these types of presentations before and typically they are very persuasive and salesy. In fact, when I saw the opening presentation video of Edward's large house and convertible Maserati car, I thought this was the same situation because I didn't know if it was really his or if this was being used to sell his services. Despite my preconceived thoughts, his presentation was very interesting because he made me feel like it's not too late to start building my finances.

I decided to approach him after his seminar and ask him to help me build my finances. I was nervous speaking to him because I was homeless, and I didn't know if he would take me seriously. Edward's reaction to my request was incredibly comforting, and he agreed to work with me. After hearing my story, he asked me for a hug and had his assistant get my contact information. Edward called me the following week for an hour-long conversation about an analysis of how to change my situation and build my finances. My savings have improved since our initial meeting.

I recommend that everyone reads this book, *Wealth Building For Beginners*, because it is a much-needed resource. People need to know that you can start from anywhere, and if you follow the process, you will get to where you want to be. It doesn't matter if you aren't currently where you want to be because what is most important is that you have a plan for accumulating wealth.

Edward, I would like to thank you and your team for transferring your systems and processes into an easy-to-follow book about building wealth for anyone to pick up off a shelf and read.

INTRODUCTION

George and I were enjoying the weather at an outdoor café on the waterfront in Washington, D.C. This was our routine on the weekends as we people watched and ate good food. George is one of my good friends. He is from the Congo, Africa, and at first glance you would think he's a movie star. He's very fit, dresses in designer clothing, and drives a convertible Mercedes Benz. I also felt like a celebrity being around George because of the attention he received from women and admiration from men. The attention was contagious; riding in a $100,000 car and walking around town dressed in high-fashion clothes made me and many others want to be around him. He looked wealthy. I wanted to look the same way because I liked the reception I received from others.

George and I were friends because he felt the same as me. I had an apartment that was a short walking distance from the waterfront in a very popular area in Washington, D.C. Some would say my lifestyle of eating out daily in restaurants and spending money traveling on vacations made me look wealthy. George had a single-family home he was renting with his wife and kids. I didn't have any kids at the time and was free as a bird. My dating life was very adventurous and unstable because of my attraction to appearance only.

I made good money and spent it on entertainment and purchases that brought immediate, albeit short-lived joy. I always felt great buying new clothes, furniture, private tables at night clubs, fancy dinners at restaurants, gifts and flowers for dates, and traveling to new countries. I felt it was now time to find my wife, settle down, and live the "good life." The emotional highs and lows of dating around made me desire to have one life partner with whom I could have a strong spiritual connection with God, great companionship, and help establish some consistency in my life.

I celebrated my 30th birthday in Miami, Florida, as large as I possibly could. I rented a beautiful hotel off the beach with great views, a private balcony, and hot tub. This was the most glamorous place I've ever seen, but I could only afford to stay there on my birthday night, and I stayed in a typical hotel for the rest of my vacation. I wasn't made of money; I was just the guy who spent everything he had for the moment.

On my birthday night, I met an Italian woman named Daniela while out dancing. We had a great time out, but she was leaving for Italy the next day. She was on the last night of her vacation in Miami before returning to her hometown of Rome, Italy.

The next day, Daniela returned to her home in Rome, and George flew out to Miami to celebrate the rest of my birthday weekend with me. It was now showtime in Miami, just like our routine weekends in Washington, D.C. We had the appearance of millionaires but were far from it. To think the thoughts that are suggested by appearances is easy, but to think truth regardless of appearances requires a discipline most don't have.

I returned home after my birthday celebration. A week later, I decided to pack my clothes in my brand-new Louis Vuitton duffel bag. I was going to fly out the next day to Rome to find Daniela again.

I remembered sitting in my skyline apartment, thinking I am ready for the next chapter. So, I decided to simply leave America and set off for a different life. I had my own business, so I didn't need anyone's permission. It wasn't a large business with full-time employees. I did consulting and planning, so it was just me, and I ran my business out of my kitchen in my city apartment. As long as I had a laptop, I could run my business from anywhere in the world.

However, I didn't have much concept of running a business. I thought as long as there is money in my business account, then I had money to spend. I also had a business credit card that had a $5,000 limit, which I referred to as my personal money as well. After I purchased my one-way ticket to Rome from Washington, D.C., I had $2,000 left in my bank account and a $5,000 limit on my credit card. In my mind, that was a total of $7,000 I had to spend and would last me a lifetime! And, of course, I could still run my business from Rome, so I thought I was wealthy and didn't have a care in the world.

Growing up as a kid, I had never seen $2,000 saved up. My dad drove a taxicab, and my mom was a court secretary. Money was always tight, and the only conversations about that topic were daily dinner table questions addressed to my dad from my mom about how the bills are going to get paid. So, I grew up thinking that the number one priority with money is finding a way to get the bills paid.

There were never any conversations about saving money or building savings accounts or investing. Investing was playing the lottery in our eyes. My parents didn't own a joint savings account. My mom was the only one in our family who had a bank account. She had one because the credit union offered her a savings account when opening up a checking account to pay bills, but nothing was in it. My dad's idea of saving was buying a gold watch, gold rings, and gold bracelets, and if he ever needed money, he could pawn those items at the pawn shop and get immediate cash for it. His concept for borrowing was that if he ever needed more funds than the pawn shop would give him, then he would borrow money from the local loan sharks with whom he built relationships.

I remember one of them named Tosski. Tosski was a 70-year-old Jewish man who often lent money to my dad. My dad was an honest, hard-working guy, and Tosski knew that he could trust him. Tosski was 30 years older than my dad. The arrangement was that Tosski would lend my dad money anytime he needed it, and the payback was a quarter on a dollar in a week's time. So if my dad had to borrow $1,000 from Tosski, my dad would have to pay back $1,250 by the next week. If my dad didn't have the whole $1,250 in a week, then he must pay at least the interest of $250 a week until the complete loan is satisfied. So that loan payback could turn into $2,000 in a month if $1,000 wasn't paid back.

Can you imagine maxing out a credit card that has a $1,000 limit and not being able to pay that $1,000 total for five months, so you pay the additional $1,000 a month minimum payment due on the loan just to keep the loan active and in good standing? By five months, you would have paid an additional $5,000 of interest plus $1,000 of principal totaling $6,000!

My dad thought he was the lucky one because he found someone that would lend him money when he really needed it. I remember him saying, "Son, be a great man and always pay people back when you say so. Your word is all you have, and if you do that, you will have more opportunity to borrow from people later. So never burn your bridges."

I was a kid, and I looked up to my father. Believe it or not, I was hoping to grow up with the same honor and eventually have powerful people around me later in life whom I could borrow from if I needed it. I had no concept that I would be taken advantage of by people, like Tosski, who majorly profited off my immediate needs.

Tosski made his money in the stock market. He was already retired when he met my dad. Their relationship lasted for 29 years before Tosski passed away. He would take the interest my dad paid him on the loans and invest them, now earning interest on the interest.

Why couldn't my dad see that and do this himself? Because he had misguided perceptions about the stock market, so he never got started. He believed he would need lots of money to get started. He had no idea who to speak with to start and no idea how to put money in the market. He thought it was simply a black hole, and once you put money in it, you can't control what it does. He also thought, "What if I need that money that I used to invest, and I can't get it back? Can the government simply reach in and take my money from this stock market whenever they need it? All of this is too much to consider. I need to go to school to be able to understand how to read the stock market. I'm too old to get started. I will look stupid if I try to explain this to my wife about how our money used for bills is now in this random stock machine that goes up and down."

My dad liked dealing with cash bills because he could see it, touch it, control where it goes, and it's easy to understand. The goal is to pile up as many cash bills as you can so you can pay your bills and put the rest of the money in your socks, pockets, mattress, and refrigerators, so you can hide it for reserves in order to pay the future bills that are due in upcoming months. In getting back to my situation in Italy, all my bills were paid, and I still had $2,000 in my bank account. I also had income still coming in from my business and $5,000 on my credit card, so I was considered wealthy by my family's standards.

What Went Wrong

I was now living in Rome, Italy, and I had sublet my beautiful apartment in Washington, D.C. If I decided not to live permanently in Italy, I wanted to have a great place in which to return.

This was April of 2008, which was an election year, Obama vs. McCain. I sublet my apartment to a guy named Boris who was a lawyer moving to Washington, D.C., because he was campaigning on McCain's team. He needed a place to stay for 10 months, so it was a good trial period for me to learn if I would permanently stay in Italy.

I found myself managing my business from overseas, as well as a tenant. I had a friend named Jami help. She was a good friend who believed in me. She was the boots on the ground for managing my business, and she was my property manager as I sublet. She didn't charge me anything to do this huge favor. She had a successful career as an IT systems manager for a major corporation, and she thought one day she would be able to take over my business too because I wasn't sure if I was going to keep it. "Who knows what Italy will bring," I thought.

Things became a disaster quickly. I was living the same style of life in Rome that I had in Washington, D.C. I didn't change my behavior. I was still going out to dinners, dancing, shopping, and traveling around Europe. I was no longer interested in Daniela because I felt that I could find a better companion. My thoughts were still based on appearances.

I was still renting an apartment in the city center. I remember paying 1,000 Euro a month and thinking it was cheap. One thousand Euro at the time was almost $2,000. Very few people paid this amount for rent in 2008 because it was considered expensive by Italian standards.

I converted my cash from dollars to Euros and never cared about the currency conversions until later. I just thought the money would always continue to come, so I didn't have a problem spending.

This spending went on for a while, but my money started to dry up. My business was having problems because it was challenging corresponding with clients on the East Coast in the States when there was a six-hour time difference. I gave my clients Jami's phone number, but she had limited capacity to assist because she had a full-time job. They would often call my cell phone when they couldn't reach Jami, and it could be after midnight in Italy.

This process went on as I started to lose clients and my income started to drop. Eventually, I had to temporarily close my business because I couldn't deliver the quality service to which my clients had become accustomed.

I remember one day I looked at my bank account and I had less than $500 total and no more income coming in. I was officially broke.

President Obama had won the election, and all I could think about was that Boris would soon leave my apartment, which means I'd have to return his security deposit of $1,500 to him. Unfortunately, I had already spent that money too. I didn't have the money to give him, so he filed a lawsuit against me and Jami in court. Jami was liable as well because I asked her to initially handle the paperwork for me since I was in Italy, and she signed her name on the form as a representative for me.

I returned to Washington, D.C., for the court date. I used my credit card to book a round-trip flight. Boris was a lawyer, so he knew all the ins and outs.

When arriving to court, I learned that Boris had changed the court date for a later time. This was a huge inconvenience because I only came for the hearing. I returned to Italy a week later and conveniently forgot about this situation.

A few months later, Jami called me and told me that she had her bank account garnished for almost $10,000. To this day, I have no idea how he was able to do that. I'm assuming because my name wasn't on the sublet contract, they couldn't get anything from me. I felt so horrible. One of my closest friends agreed to do me a favor and help sublet my apartment, and now she was penalized $10,000. Jami is a short Vietnamese lady who is always loyal to her friends. How could I do this to her? She was very upset with me, understandably so, and her husband was infuriated with her for helping me. I ruined one of my strongest friendships and resources because of my bad habits with spending.

I promised Jami I would pay her back. It felt like every time I saved a little bit of money, then something would happen that would require that money I had saved. For example, I moved into a cheaper apartment and had to use the money I had saved up to pay for a deposit. Then I would save up a little money again and I would have to use it for fixing my motorcycle because it broke down and it was my only source of transportation. I saved up again after that and then I was forced to spend it because I needed to buy a business license so I could open a business in Italy.

A groundbreaking moment for me happened shortly after I purchased my business license. My dad had been struggling with diabetes, and he needed his foot amputated. He needed some money to help with his hospital bills and to help with keeping Mom afloat while he was in the hospital. It was a very dark moment in my life because my dad is everything to me. My dad sacrificed a lot to give me a great future, as he drove taxicabs, risking his life to put food on our table.

The lowest point of my life was when he asked me to borrow some money for that emergency, and I didn't have any money to help him. He never asked me for money before that moment because he always assumed the role of the giver to his family, and the one time that my hero needed someone to rescue him, I couldn't.

He and my mom ended up making ends meet because he was able to borrow money from one of his sisters, other family members, and his friends, and all I could do was thank them for helping. I was powerless, embarrassed, and ashamed.

That was my breakthrough moment because I looked at the flashy life that I displayed to everyone, yet I didn't have any real wealth to show for my success. I only had symbols of wealth with my material purchases.

I will never leave my senior citizen dad alone and vulnerable in the jungle again. At the time, I was a weak gazelle trying to protect my family, but I promised myself that I would become a strong lion with my finances soon.

SECTION 1:
The 3 Poisonous P's That Can Block You from Achieving Wealth: Personal Obstacles to Overcome

CHAPTER 1
Habit #1: Perception

The purpose of this book is not to provide some big general philosophy that you agree with, but then not know what to do with the philosophy. Rather, it is to provide practical, comprehensive, step-by-step instructions that will get you closer to building wealth. It doesn't matter your starting point.

"Baby steps count too, as long as you are going forward" - Reverend Cecil Williams.

When you add all those baby steps up one day, you might be surprised how far you have gotten. This book is about practical steps you can do today if you want to increase your chances of being wealthy.

Before getting into the formulas, processes, and vehicles needed to achieve wealth, which comes in Chapter 4, we need to first prevent the roadblocks that could stop us from using the advancement tools I will provide later. I call these roadblocks the **Poisonous P's.**

The first one is perception. George and I were both home renters, with flashy lifestyles of designer clothes, luxury cars, and dining in fancy cafes where we could be seen. We wanted others to see us with these "wealth indicators" because we believed it would attract other people to want to be around us and that could lead to better life opportunities. For George, the opportunities he was looking for were business invitations. By looking successful, he assumed he would get into the circles of successful people. The circles he got into were people who wanted to be around him because they too can look good next to him in hopes of attracting a significant business proposal.

What he didn't realize was that all the people in those circles were posing exactly like he was. Just like he was attracting people who fall victim to appearances, he was also a victim of appearances because he thought he had figured out what wealthy people look like.

I wasn't any better. I applied these same "wealth indicators" too because I was looking for opportunities to date and possibly find my wife. When growing up, I was the awkward-looking skinny kid with braces who played classical piano. So, dating was challenging throughout my life until I began working on the perception others have of me. I do not recommend anyone do that because I lost myself in the process of trying to look and be what other people think I should look like and be like.

Later, after inserting in the superficial "wealth indicators" of white teeth, muscles, high-fashion clothes, a waterfront apartment, high-value friends who drive a convertible Mercedes Benz, afternoon coffee at outdoor cafés, putting my credit card down for a bill before even looking at the bill, and a cuddly dog as a status symbol, dating got a whole lot easier because women wanted to be around me. They weren't aware that all that stuff wasn't real. That wasn't the real me. By the way, George's convertible Mercedes was used, and it always had mechanical problems. But when it was working, it looked nicely polished, and we looked good in it.

So, as I was dating, I had to keep up this perception others had of me, and it became very expensive. My dates would often wonder why they would only see me once every month or longer and that was because I didn't have the money to keep up that image. **It takes a lot of money to make it look like you have a lot of money!**

There is a perception you should never let people know you are broke because people will not want to be around you. The misconception is that it's better to try to show others you are wealthy when you aren't. Well, remember it takes a lot of money to make it look like you have a lot of money. Therefore, if you try to show people you are wealthy, then eventually you will become broke trying to keep up that image.

So, the question is, do you **a)** try to show people you are wealthy when you are not and eventually end up broke, or do you **b)** show people you are broke, but you are working to become wealthy? The answer to this question is very obvious. You can't fake authenticity. If you act like you already have it when you don't, who is going to help you get it?

Wealthy people love a good underdog story! What I have learned in my years of owning a financial firm is wealthy people love helping other people acquire wealth. If you ever meet a wealthy person, ask them one question—how did they become so wealthy and successful? Then, have a seat, because they will talk for days. Not only do most people love talking about themselves, but the only thing greater than having wealth is sharing the wealth.

Now, I'm not talking about helping charity cases either. The key difference is working to become wealthy. Many people are completely content not being wealthy, and that is fine too. No one is going to help change your situation if you aren't making an earnest effort to improve it yourself.

Poor people, on the other hand, do not want to help anyone but themselves because many have scarcity mindsets. They fear it will run out. They think if it's given to you, then they will have less for themselves.

Have you ever met a person who has the potential to introduce you to the same opportunity they have, but they don't because they fear you'll take what's meant for them? Somehow, whatever opportunity they were given, it is only enough for them and no one else. They do not want you to eat off their plate. So, they tell you, "Let me get in first and then after I have eaten, I will try to bring you in because now I'm too full and can't eat anymore. And when I get hungry again, I will leave you once again and eat as much as I can and, if you are still my friend, I might consider bringing you to that table as well,"—as though they are doing you a favor that is costing them.

Wealthy people don't mind spreading the wealth. They think in abundance. There is always more where that came from. So, if you answered the above question with option **b),** then you are correct. You will have a much higher chance of becoming wealthy by being authentic. With option **a),** who are you really fooling? It's not a coincidence that George's behaviors and mannerisms put him in circles with other people who were posing just like him.

Where do we get these thoughts from? We hear it all the time. "Never let them see you sweat." Perhaps that was a survival technique used years ago with our parents and their parents. If people showed a weakness, then that weakness would be exploited. But it could also be pride, which we will discuss in more detail later.

I remember being a kid, and we needed money to pay the electricity bill because it was going to get cut off the next day. I was going to call my aunt to ask for help since she seemed to be very well off. She owned a successful funeral home and besides, we are family. When I approached my dad and told him about my grand idea to simply ask my aunt, someone would have thought that a nuclear explosion happened in my house! My dad was furious and heated. He said, "Never let people know our personal business. You will shame our family." I said, "But, Dad, how will I shame our family, if we need help, shouldn't we ask for help?" He said, "No." So, he believed it was better to suffer than to ask for help.

Eventually, he got the money from Tosski, which I didn't understand. It was better for my dad to pay an additional 25% weekly than to borrow the money from a family member and only pay back the principal with zero interest. Now as an adult, I can understand being self-sufficient, because we should have sources that we built for emergencies, but when your perceptions and viewpoints start to become heavily damaging to your finances, it's a problem. My dad was wired for ancient survival techniques.

We do not only want to survive; we want to thrive! Below is a diagram from Eugene Mitchell's book *Closing the Racial Wealth Gap*. Eugene is a friend and founder of the $50 Billion Community

Empowerment Movement. Although Eugene's case studies were with the African American populations, I found this diagram can also be true for other nationalities and races. This diagram he designed is not universal and does not pertain to all. It illustrates the differences in habits in 12 key areas of people who are accustomed to having money (**Old money**) and people who recently received money or are trying to get it (**New money**):

	Old Money	*New Money*
Clothing:	Own well-made clothing, maintained over time. Designer items are often years old. Quality comes first.	Stylish. Lots of new current-season designer-label items. Can only wear something once publicly.
Cars:	Cars are transportation. They aren't meant to attract attention. "Maintain something well, and it will last forever."	Your car is your rolling net-worth statement. "You are what you drive."
Home Décor:	Happy with period furniture and stately antiques. As stated in the television show *Downton Abbey*, "Your lot buys it, my lot inherits it."	Keep current with trends. Work with interior designers. Invented "fashion furniture," disposing of it every few years.

	Old Money	*New Money*
Homes:	Properties may be large, but not necessarily. Often handed down or inherited homes family members grew up in. Have no mortgages.	Properties are large, often an over extension to keep up with the Joneses. Used interest-only loans in the mortgage bubble to get bigger homes beyond means.
Investing:	Capital preservation, while keeping up with inflation, is their primary objective. They are stewards of their family's wealth for future generations.	They speculate to accumulate. More cavalier, short sighted, and open to risk.
Eat in/out:	Do eat out, but largely like to entertain at home. Do their own cooking. Meals can be simple. Chili is fine. However, enjoy throwing formal receptions as well. Own all the entertaining accouterments, which were often wedding presents.	Primarily entertain by dining out. Couples split the check down the middle. The grander the kitchen, the less likely it's ever used.

	Old Money	*New Money*
Spending Habits:	Surprisingly, wealthy people often come across as cheap. They like getting a good deal, but don't talk about it. They never talk about how much they've paid- and might actually complain about high prices. Openly bragging about how much they have paid is seen as lowbrow and vulgar.	Get the biggest and most expensive of whatever they're buying to make a statement. Splurge is a favorite verb.
Travel:	Are well-traveled, but don't announce it directly. When talking amongst themselves, they know details of streets in major cities, what it's like to sail into a harbor, or what are the must-see current theater productions—from New York's Broadway to London's West End.	It's not only where you went, but also how much you spent, the name of the hotel, and size of the suite.

	Old Money	*New Money*
Charity:	They see supporting the arts and cultural institutions as an obligation that comes with wealth.	More interested in naming opportunities that reflect back to self than supporting the cultural institution's underlying mission.
Hired help:	May have a nanny or housekeeper, but most don't hire full-time staff. Cook meals and serve guests themselves. Many clean their own homes too.	The hiring of staff is a conspicuous display of wealth. They don't clean their own home. Complain about the difficulty of finding good help.
The Second Home:	Have summer houses at the shore or in the mountains. Working spouse stays in the city weekdays and returns to second home on weekends.	Where you spend the summer is important. Rent a house in the Hamptons or on the Vineyard. Let everyone know and invite people to visit
Talking About Wealth:	Very strategic and methodical in passing investment advice on to the next generation, while the family is seated at the dinner table	They talk about spending constantly

All those things that George and I tried to get so that other people saw us as being wealthy were short-term and they didn't last.

I was renting an apartment and George was renting a house that he didn't own. Renting is designed to be only for a period of time and when that time period expires, the price increases and you leave. Or, some people will rent for years if they have no other choice. I never understood that. If your rent is $2,000 and you stay there for a year, that is $24,000. Two years would run you $48,000. Is that not enough for a down payment on a beautiful home? I have seen clients that walked into my office who have been renting for 10 years or more! In my opinion, it is like dumping $240,000 into an ocean because you do not have anything to show for it. If you have a landlord and you drive a Mercedes, then you have a major problem. Your perception needs heavy adjustment.

The wealthy people who have come through the doors of my financial practice typically and unconsciously use this formula. The terms of any **financial purchase have to be less than < (ROI +FV)**. ROI is return on investment. FV is future value. Whenever they buy into something, it has to be less than what they think they are going to get out of it.

This is where most people fail. You should never do something based on the ROI. That's how people ruin their finances because in life you must include future value in order to achieve wealth. When buying something ask yourself, "Will this benefit me in 5 years, 10 years, 15 years? Will this purchase serve me later?" If the answer is "no," then don't buy it.

When you start thinking about future value, you will find that you start making very different decisions. Buy future value things and create friendships with future value people. If you look past the short-term perception, the long-term value will change your life.

When you buy something, ask yourself, "Does this decision support me building wealth, not just what I think I need to have now because I want it, or so someone else can potentially give wealth to me?" Those who make decisions based on ROI are not looking over the fence to wealth.

Remember, baby steps. The cavalry isn't coming to save you. You have to build it yourself. This book will teach you how to be further thinking in your pursuit of wealth building.

"Congratulations! Because you are taking your first steps toward expanding your wealth by purchasing and reading my book, I will gift you a complimentary consultation with my team of licensed professionals and provide you with our Wealth Starter Kit. Wedge™ folder included! Go to https://edwardrwilliams.com/wealth-kit/ to receive my gift. Let's build your wealth!" – Edward

Summary

Poor people do not want to help anyone but themselves because many have scarcity mindsets. They fear their money will run out. Wealthy people don't mind spreading the wealth. They think in abundance. You will have a much higher chance of becoming wealthy by being authentic. Write down some of the things you could do to avoid having the fear of not having enough money.

We learned about the differences between "new money" and "old money." The main difference is those who have been accustomed to having money tend to take care of things better, are often frugal, and live a more modest lifestyle. You would not know they are wealthy by looking at them. Make a list of purchases you made or avoided to get better value for your dollar. Develop better spending guidelines to avoid the frivolous spending trap.

When buying something, ask yourself if this will benefit me in 5 years, 10 years, 15 year, etc.? Will this purchase serve me later? If the answer is "no," then don't buy it.

CHAPTER 2
Habit #2: Procrastination

Generally, if you are assigned a large task such as passing a university final exam, reading a novel, or building a house, you typically do or prepare a little bit each day until it's all completed by the deadline so that you can manage everything. This is what I am told.

For some reason, my mind doesn't work that way. When I was in business school, if I had a final exam assigned on September 2nd that was scheduled for February 6th, my process typically went like this: In September, I would be given a study schedule outline of what to study each month until the exam in February. I would have every intention of following that schedule so I can tackle a little bit each day by not making it harder later.

Unfortunately, in September life happens, preventing me from following that schedule, so I simply reassess October's workload by adding September's materials—no problem at all. Then October arrives and I realize it's my birthday month, so I have to celebrate the whole month by relaxing and doing low-stress activities. So I will have to just work harder than usual in November because I'll strategically push September and October's workload into November.

Now that November is here, I finally open my books to begin studying for my exam in February, but minutes later, I realize it's Sunday and football is on, and since it only comes on once a week, I could start studying another day.

The days turn into weeks, and now December is here. No need to worry, because I still have two whole months before the exam. Now I'm going to have to work very hard, but I made it this far in my life by working hard and this is not new to me. I can do it because I still have two whole months.

The first week of December my friend Yousef from Egypt calls me and reminds me that New Year's Eve is coming up and we haven't planned anything yet. New Year's Eve is the biggest celebration of the year and requires extensive planning. So I jump on it and start planning our big New Year's Eve adventure because life is short, and you only live once. Who knows what will happen later? New Year's Eve might not come around again, so we need to make sure that we celebrate in style.

Then, I look up and it's the end of January, and I have one week to prepare for this exam. Where did the time go? Now I must study September, October, November, December, and January's materials all in one week!

Panic sets in. I got maybe seven hours of sleep the whole week, staying up for almost three days straight studying with boatloads of caffeine from coffee and Mountain Dew soda. Mountain Dew's bromine ingredient is now banned in 100 countries. It is considered a toxic chemical that has been linked to all kinds of health concerns, including organ system damage, birth defects, schizophrenia, and hearing loss. This is the stuff I was drinking to stay awake and study. I was doing stuff the human body shouldn't have any business doing, and I definitely would not recommend anyone push themselves to these limits.

I'm not going to say if I passed the exam or not because luck has no relevance to the story. This book is about providing step-by-step instructions that will get you closer to achieving wealth and not using luck and hope as a core strategy. I was clearly a procrastinator.

Procrastination is one of the Poisonous P's that I am an expert in because I was a master procrastinator. In my financial practice, I now tell all my clients that the word **"someday" is a disease that will take your dreams of financial wealth away.**

I can explain what goes on in the minds of procrastinators. I could show someone an unbelievable analysis to drastically increase their chances of obtaining wealth, and they will take that folder and say, "Thank you so much for showing me this, I will implement this strategy (someday) soon." Then I see them 10 years later, and they are in the same exact financial position because they haven't started yet, and now they will have to do double and triple just to catch up.

Just like me pushing September through January study load to February, their cycle will continue until they are 55 years old with nothing saved. The dream of being able to retire by age 65 has now gone away and working hard for the rest of their lives until they die is becoming a reality.

To the other procrastinators who are reading this book, I believe we love instant gratification. We procrastinate because we want instant gratification. If building wealth is the goal, then we want wealth tomorrow. We typically live for the moment with no memory of the past. We care most about things being easy, no stress, and fun.

Here is a breakthrough statement for all the procrastinators with obtaining wealth as the goal: **Sometimes you have to fight that urge of doing things that are easy, no stress, and fun and force yourselves to do things that are harder, stressful, and less pleasant for the sake of obtaining the big goal**.

Procrastinators have a problem with this the most. When a procrastinator is doing something other than the important task at hand, it is because they want things to be easy, no stress, and fun. That distracting activity that they choose to do is not real fun because later they realize it's unearned and experience feelings of guilt, anxiety, dread, and self-hatred.

Panic can be a healthy response to battling procrastination, like when I realized I had a week left to study for my business school final exam. Panic is like those white blood cells that come in to protect your body when you have an illness. Sometimes they can protect you, and sometimes they can't and you die. White blood cells form to help fight an illness and disease that infects your body.

People panic when it is the last line of defense against procrastination. It's a risky strategy to wait until you panic because sometimes the pressure can be too great to overcome. This is the procrastinators process that circles over and over:

- Important task assigned that will improve overall situation
- Delay the task by choosing an activity that's easy, no stress, and fun
- Feelings of guilt, anxiety, dread, self-hatred settle in
- Panic
- Return to important task assigned that will improve overall situation
- Delay the task by choosing an activity that's easy, no stress, and fun, etc.

My task assigned that would improve my overall situation was to pass my final exam. There was a deadline of February 6th. When there is a deadline, the negative effects of procrastination are limited and contained because the task assigned will eventually end.

What if there was no deadline to the task assigned? For example, what if your task was to lose weight, make an impact on the world, or build wealth? None of those tasks assigned have deadlines. The effects of procrastination could be very detrimental because it would continue to strengthen, and the negative feelings of guilt, anxiety, dread, and self-hatred will pile up over time and magnify. Panic, your last line of defense, might not ever arrive until it's too late because there is no deadline.

I have sat down with so many people in their 60s and 70s who wanted to build wealth but never got started. They have intense frustration and anger with what procrastinating has done to their lives. The frustration is not that they couldn't achieve wealth, it's that they couldn't even get started chasing wealth. Without a real deadline, procrastination can be like a long-distance foot race runner with no finish line. The rationale becomes, "Who wants to keep running forever, so why start?"

"Procrastination can be the source of a lot of long-term unhappiness and regrets." - Tim Urban, blogger, "Inside the Mind of a Master Procrastinator."

Procrastination has made people feel like a spectator of their own lives. That is why shows such as *Lifestyles of the Rich and Famous*, *Real Housewives*, and *Million Dollar Listing* are popular, especially to procrastinators because it's easy, less stress, and fun to watch and, they become spectators.

For a long time, I had a difficult time building wealth with younger clients because they would view the extended time horizon as an infinity of years in front of them, so it was challenging to incentivize them to start building now. Their philosophy was to do what is comfortable, easy, and no stress now. Why should they have any type of intensity or serious focus because they have forever to build wealth? Just like me having five months to study for my exam—why start studying in the first month?

I remembered asking one of my younger clients named Sarah that if building wealth is the goal, does she agree starting earlier would increase her chances of achieving the goal? She said, "Yes, Edward, that is obvious." Then I would say, "Okay, well, let's start saving, protecting, and investing now because you agree that your chances of achieving wealth would increase if we started now." Then she would say, "Well, what if I die before I had a chance to spend my money, and I wasted my life by saving and building? Then I said, "Good point, so let's weigh the options because anything you do half-heartedly in life will produce half-hearted results."

Option #1 is you save and build now, and later have much more money to spend and enjoy for the rest of your life. Option #2 is you don't save and try to enjoy the little money you have now and risk running out of money later. Option #3 is you save and build now but die before you reach the finish line of achieving wealth.

I asked which option is the worst and which option is the best if they come true. She said #3 is the worst because all her saving would have been for nothing because she dies and never reaches wealth.

She said, "Edward, I have an option that is better than all three. How about I enjoy the little bit of money I have now while I am young, and later when I get older, I can start saving and investing so that I do not eventually run out of money?"

I said, "Sarah, you already agreed that starting to build and save earlier would increase your chances of achieving your goal of wealth building. Wouldn't you want to set yourself up with the greatest chances possible of achieving your goals?"

She said, "Yeah, you are right. I just wouldn't want to miss out on the things that I can have now."

Sarah, like many other people, wants instant gratification, which translates into wanting to speed on the highway of life without any preparation for the trip. You don't plan for any unexpected bumps in life, and you end up running out of gas at the worst possible time.

A children's story comes to mind when I think about Sarah. It's called *The Ant and the Grasshopper*. The story is about a grasshopper who came to the ants begging for food and shelter because she danced and played all summer long and didn't put in the work to prepare herself for winter. In contrast, the ants worked hard all summer, and little by little, they saved up for a harsh winter. They prepared food and built shelter, and the grasshopper who danced and had fun had nothing at the end. So, the moral of the story is, if you choose to dance and spend money now because you want things to be easy, no stress, and fun, then you might be left with nothing later when it really counts since you never took the steps to prepare early enough.

Sarah's vision of her finances is stuck to this day. A lot of the reason why people procrastinate and don't take real, practical, common-sense efforts toward building wealth is that they don't see themselves wealthy in the future. They haven't visualized what that would feel like yet. They think, "Oh, that would be nice if I were wealthy," but there is a difference between, "Oh that would be nice if I were wealthy," and "I own my dream of being wealthy." You don't luck into that. There is no casual approach to that. You have to feel it, see it, and sense it happening to you so you can step into it.

People fear efforts could be wasted saving and building now at the present moment because they might not get to the finish line of real wealth building. I remind them that it's never about the destination, it is always about the journey. There is an old wise saying that the harder the struggle, the more glorious the triumph.

"Success is a journey, not a destination. The doing is often more important than the outcome" - Arthur Ashe.

Who taught them it's about the destination? Building wealth may not always be good-looking. It doesn't look like a lot, but it feels like a lot. It is simply little inches, steps forward, and incremental advancements. Procrastinators want the instant gratification. They want the destination immediately, and the day that they don't feel the destination is near, they become discouraged.

The most important thing about wealth building is starting now. Procrastinators want their dream of achieving wealth to be delivered like an Amazon package.

What are you willing to sacrifice in order to achieve your goal of building wealth? **Are you willing to sacrifice quick, short-term pleasures of purchases for long-term financial success and stability?**

Summary

We procrastinate because we want instant gratification. Sometimes you have to fight that urge of doing things that are easy, no stress, and fun and force yourselves to do things that are harder, stressful, and less pleasant for the sake of obtaining the big goal. Make a list of things you procrastinated on and how it impacted your wealth.

There is an old wise saying that, the harder the struggle, the more glorious the triumph. Identify three areas in your life you had the most struggle. Find and engage with a mentor in each of those areas. Your mentors could be people who have overcome the struggles you have experienced. The feedback you get could help you avoid the same struggles as well as provide you with insight into how to do better.

CHAPTER 3
Habit #3: Pride

My financial firm was really growing, and we were helping more people than ever. I was inducted into this organization called Million Dollar Round Table and the ceremony was in Australia. The organization selects the top advisors in the world. It's generally the top 1%, based on revenue and production. I was honored and very proud to be admitted into this organization, as it was a great accomplishment to receive all the plaques, certificates, and recognitions.

Upon returning to work in America from my trip, my cousin Michelle reached out to me on the phone to congratulate me, as she saw a magazine editorial of my company. She said, "Congratulations cousin, I see you are really doing great things for your clients! Would you mind reviewing my husband's and my retirement plan? We have some things in place but I'm not sure it's enough because we never want to worry about running out of money and re-entering the job force by working at a supermarket while in our 70s." I said, "Sure, let's pick a date and since you are family, I can come over to your home where it's more comfortable for you, instead of you coming to my office. That way, we can also share a dinner and I can see your beautiful kids." We set the appointment, and I drove over to Michelle's house a month later.

As I'm entering Michelle's home, she sits me down in the living room very gingerly. I could tell something was wrong because she wasn't as excited as she was when we spoke on the phone about this a month ago. I asked her if everything was okay, and she said, "Not really, Edward, because we won't be able to discuss our finances today. I didn't cancel our appointment because I still wanted you to have an opportunity to see my kids and have dinner with us."

I said, "Why do you no longer want me to help with your retirement planning?" She said because it caused a lot of problems with her husband. He got very angry when she told him I will help them with their finances. He said, "We don't need any help from your baby cousin. I am in charge of taking care of our household finances and you don't need to be telling people our business. Why don't you ask him to show you how much money he has saved and tell him I can help him get to a better place, like us."

Wow! Michelle told me all of this and didn't hold back. She wanted me to know that she didn't have anything to do with this decision and she was very apologetic.

Too much pride can ruin your chances of obtaining wealth. Many people often think pride is a positive thing. You should always be proud of yourself, but too much of it is not good. This is different than having a healthy self-image.

Michelle's husband clearly had too much pride. Pride is a belief that you are superior to others. Pride makes you compare yourself to other people, and it depends on you being better than another person. You will try to save face so that you can keep from exposing yourself to other people for the sake of keeping up with appearances. There should be no shame in needing someone to talk to or someone else's help, especially if that someone is a professional like myself, who has dedicated decades of their life being a student to wealth building, and Michelle's husband wants to build wealth.

It is okay not to be an expert in everything. I wonder if Michelle invited an aircraft pilot over to their house to discuss organizing a private flight to a paradise destination, would her husband refuse the conversation with the pilot because he considered himself a better aviator since he has been on planes before and doesn't need any help getting to their paradise destination? I don't think he would oppose that conversation with the pilot because he's not expected to know how to fly a plane, but he is expected to know how to financially save, and he is embarrassed that it's not done properly. I suspect that it wasn't done properly because if it was, then you wouldn't have any problems showing someone else your great work.

When people have done well saving, they love coming into my office showing me the number of zeros behind their number on their 401(k) or IRA statements. It's so funny because they are waving that piece of paper around like it's a flag or something. They can't wait for me to ask for it.

I remember one of my elderly clients named Mary entered my office with her financial documents in a folder and pulled out her IRA statement so she could hold the loose statement in her other hand. Mary is a very frail and adorable older woman who is always happy and filled with joy. I walked out to our office lobby and saw her sitting down in the reception area with her large crown church hat that was probably half the size of her whole body, with her statement in her hand and her folder in her lap. When she saw me, she stood up, and said, "Mr. Williams, I brought my IRA statement along with the other statements you requested in my folder you gave me."

Mary's IRA statement was her badge of honor, and she was very proud and grateful for her hard work in building her IRA. She didn't think she was better than anyone else, and she wasn't too proud to consider help with improving it because she understood it could fade.

I have also seen people with wealth lose it because of too much pride. Knowledge is the enemy of pride. It is like water that falls from the sky. Knowledge intensifies the direction of people as water intensifies the direction of plants. When water is poured on a bitter plant, it becomes more bitter. When water is poured on a sweet plant, it becomes sweeter. A person can be given knowledge by someone else and become more bitter and defensive, or a person can be given knowledge by someone else and grow and improve.

Having too much pride can prevent you from telling someone else about your doubts, past mistakes, or insecurities. It can lead to you feeling very isolated with your hidden issue. **Pride can be a mask for shame and insecurity, all dependent on you being richer, or more accomplished, older, or smarter than someone else.** It's based on an artificial comparison.

Don't base your sense of self on a concept in your mind of a set of conditions staying the same because things change. Basing your sense of self on something that will one day change means that when change happens, you will feel empty because those conditions have changed, and you are no longer who you used to be.

For example, Michelle's husband always saw me as the younger cousin. He saw me going to undergraduate school and business school studying about finances while he was working and making money in the real world. So, he was the expert in building money at the time, but circumstances changed, and I later gained more knowledge and experience in the area of building wealth. So, he could no longer have that superior frame and he tried to save face to keep me or Michelle from knowing that he is no longer the stronger one in this field.

Don't be prideful, be grateful like Mary because things could change. Act with humility in all circumstances. Don't be a victim of this disease of having too much pride because you will be unable to accept the truth and knowledge that promotes growth and improvement. Below are some red flag indicators of having too much pride:

1. **Bad listener.** They are not willing to listen to what you have to say. They know it all. You can't reason with them because they don't consider other people's opinions.
2. **Unteachable.** No matter how hard you try, they just won't learn. They have a hard time accepting correction or criticism. They become defensive. If you are unteachable, that means no growth can happen.
3. **Oversensitivity.** They have oversensitivity because they are easily hurt and easily irritated. It's like having an infected wound that becomes sensitive.
4. **Bitterness.** They have a hard time letting go of their hurts.

It's important to know you can't get help with an issue until you admit there is a problem. You are NOT viewed as weak if you ask for help. There is a popular saying that pride comes before the fall. That means people will die starving because of their pride. It makes you blind to your own faults and blind to correction. You are quick to point out someone else's faults before looking at yours because it distracts you from the pain of looking at your own faults. Pride can be healthy, like my client Mary's spirit of pride.

**"The spirit of pride says that wealth comes from hard work."
-Dave Ramsey.**

It's a cause and effect. There is a theme throughout this book that says start now, build slowly, and spend later.

As a financial professional, there is nothing that bothers me more than people who don't plant anything and then sit back and say, "I hope the government planted some potatoes for later!" You have got to put in the hard work so you can enjoy it later. That is healthy pride, and there is nothing wrong with that. You have a truthful awareness and knowledge of knowing you're not solely responsible for the harvest you accumulated later, and you act with humility. There are always other people who help you along the way. You aren't thinking that you did all the work, so you deserve to look down on other people who don't have what you do. You may have planted the crops, but it was the farmers who managed it, and the sun provided the energy so it can grow, and the rain provided the nutrients for it to stay alive.

If those analogies are clear, then here is another one. You must prep and cook the food first before you can eat it. Financial wealth is much the same way.

If you build your money the correct way, then I believe you deserve to enjoy it. You have earned it.

I do lots of presentations in the church about pride because I am a man of faith. I hear all the opposing views on having wealth. Some will say that wealth is not good to have because it comes from the devil, and it is evil. Do not fall victim to that trap. I have seen people who aren't so knowledgeable about the words of scripture take a slice-and-dice of it to make a point. I remembered meeting someone who tried to make me feel bad about having a nice car. I found it interesting because I donated and gave back to the church and other charities weekly, more than he has all year. I am not going to write much about this subject but be cautious of jealous and envious people. Jealous people want what you have, and envious people don't think they will ever be able to get what you have, so they don't want you to have it either.

The moral of the story is, wealthy people aren't evil and poor people aren't holy. There are good and bad people in both categories. Gain a healthy self-image of pride through hard work and remain open to knowledge.

Summary

Too much pride can ruin your chances of obtaining wealth. Many people often think pride is a positive thing. You should always be proud of yourself, but too much of it is not good. Write out a few excuses you may be clinging to when it comes to having too much pride to admit you need help with something.

Try not to be too proud. Make a list of some areas you are not doing great with your wealth plan and make it a point to share this with your financial advisor. You are NOT viewed as weak if you ask for help.

SECTION 2:

Transcend Yourself by Building a Wedge.
Wealth Building Starts Here!

CHAPTER 4:
Insurance

Now that we got the Poisonous P's out of the way, which are the major things that can block you from building wealth, the runway is all clear for taking off. If you notice, lack of money is not one of the Poisonous P's. It's my personal opinion that as long as you have income coming in, it is enough. I have seen people who make over half a million dollars a year have less net worth and less surplus than someone who makes $50,000 a year. How is this possible? I know that is hard to believe, but I wouldn't have believed it either unless I saw it.

It's actually quite basic. How much is your net worth? Net worth is simply how much you own minus how much you owe. If the high earner has purchased many things and has mountains of debt, more debt than the value of the things that she has owned, than her net worth is negative. If she spends more than she saves, then she also has a deficit. If the guy who earns $50,000 a year doesn't spend much and owns more than he owes in debt, then his net worth is positive, and if he spends less than he makes, he has a surplus. That is Finance 101. It's not how much you make, it's all about how much you save.

When people tell me they make a lot of money, that means absolutely nothing to me because it's not the most important factor in building wealth. I'm not naïve either. I completely understand having more income coming in could increase your speed, but it's important to know that your speed can increase in either direction—either faster backwards or faster forwards. Everyone remembers the old fable, *The Tortoise and the Hare*. Slow and steady wins the race.

So the formula for building wealth is:

- Protect the income that is currently coming in the household.
- Save a quarter of what you make.
- Grow what is saved.
- Pass on what is left over to loved ones, so they too won't have to start over with nothing.

That formula is like platinum gold. I was never told this as a kid or young adult. For the readers who have kids, please give a copy of this book to your kids. Awareness is the key.

This coronavirus pandemic has exposed a lot of people. It's very easy now to see the differences between the haves and the have nots.

Through my work with a team of financial professionals, we determined that a major difference between many of the haves and have nots is a simple wedge. **A wedge is a triangular shaped tool that is used to separate two objects; it first holds an object in place while lifting the object up along the way.** It looks like a door stopper that you put on the ground to hold the door in place. It has grids along the way, and the more force applied, the further up that grid the object goes. What if that object is you, as you travel your journey to building financial wealth? What tools do we need that will first hold our finances in place, preventing us from going backwards, and then gradually drive us up toward our financial destination?

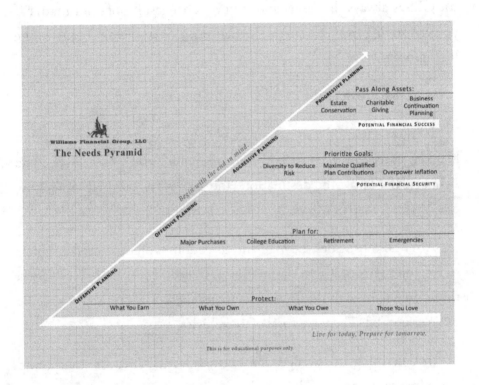

Diagram 1A

In this diagram, you can visualize the wedge triangle shape. The above arrow going up reads, "Begin with the end in mind." If the goal is to build wealth, then you have to exactly define what that is. What does that look like? If it's a number, what is that number? Once you know that number, then simply start from wherever you currently are in relation to the goal and build your way up to that.

For example, when using a tool such as GPS to get to your destination, the first thing it asks you is to enter the address of where you are going. Then, after it knows your destination, it pulls your current location and calculates a route for you to get there. The process for GPS is always the same, and it never changes; it does not matter if you are driving from New York to California or from your house to the local grocery store.

A wedge provides the route to wealth building.

I know some of you are probably thinking, "Oh great, another blanket statement such as eat your vegetables and you will become stronger. If I know the destination, and I know where I am now, how can I use this map of the wedge? Where is the car?"

After GPS provides the map and directions, you now need a vehicle to get you there, or if that destination is Italy and you are in New York, then you will need multiple vehicles to get there. Let's get to the specific vehicles needed. There is a total of 10 vehicles.

In describing this wedge, the bottom reads, "Live for today, and plan for tomorrow." This wedge design is not intended to stop someone from enjoying today while planning for tomorrow. Remember the Arthur Ashe quote from chapter two: "Success is a journey, not a destination. The doing is often more important than the outcome." So, enjoy the process.

The bottom of the wedge starts with the foundation of protection. Just like anything else that is built, you must start at the ground or the base and ensure that it's very strong to build on top of. With a weak base or foundation, everything else is subject to collapse.

Since wealth building is the goal, how do I complete step 1 of the formula, which is to first make sure to protect the income that is currently coming in the household? The most inexpensive way to do that is with insurance plans, without having to worry about putting aside hundreds of thousands of dollars to self-insure.

Insurance is a dirty word because it does the roll-your-sleeves-up manual labor but doesn't get the credit for it. It is like the construction worker vs. interior designer. The worker builds the foundation so the house can stay standing and not fall while you are decorating and making it look gorgeous.

There are four types of insurances needed to protect what you earn, own, owe, and those you love. You don't want your income or the things you own to go away. You don't want creditors to come after the debt you owe, and you don't want loved ones who rely on you to suffer if you're no longer providing financially.

Before I moved to Italy from Washington, D.C., I did investment banking for Merrill Lynch. I started off interning with the private client sector in Washington, D.C., then moved to the mergers and acquisitions group within the investment banking division on Wall Street in New York, and later ended up in the real estate group within the investment banking division in London, England. That part of my life was very stressful. I developed high blood pressure. It's believed this was caused by the stress and the nature of the business. High blood pressure also runs in my family. So, I returned to America because I wanted a less stressful environment. I wanted life to be easy and fun.

The strangest thing happened upon returning. For some reason, my blood pressure got higher weeks after being in Washington, D.C. I don't know if it was all the sodium in the foods in the United States or what, but I had to go to the emergency room. While in the emergency room, the doctor gave me a pill, and my blood pressure lowered. I left the hospital hours later.

I was fine, until I received the bill months later in the mail for that emergency room visit. Unbelievably, it was thousands of dollars! Just riding in an ambulance cost almost $10,000. I had to pay all that money out of pocket because I didn't have health insurance. I thought because I lived overseas that I didn't need it. It was a bone-headed decision on my part, and it will never happen again.

Always make sure you have **health insurance**. These plans can be pennies on a dollar with assistance such as the Affordable Care Act (ACA), also known as Obamacare. The monthly premiums that are paid on insurance plans are small compared to how much you will pay out of pocket if something health-related happens to you. Many employers offer health insurance plans. Health savings account (HSA) and a flexible spending account (FSA) are both tax-advantaged accounts that allow an individual to save specifically for medical costs. A significant difference between (FSA) and (HSA) is that an individual controls an HSA and allows contributions to roll over while FSA's are less flexible and owned by an employer. HSA's are not a standard savings account and are only available to people who have a high-deductible health plan. You can also deduct the year's contributions from your taxes when you file. The goal is to avoid unnecessary money from leaving your household, so it's better to pay the small premiums to protect the larger amount from getting deducted if there is a health-related emergency.

Imagine you are driving your car to work, and you must travel on the highway. While you are driving and feeling good while singing to the music on the radio, a teenager who is in the car behind you is texting and driving. He doesn't look up until it's too late and smash! He runs into the back of you and throws you out of the car. The ambulance comes immediately and the doctors save you from dying. The doctor makes you feel a little better hours later by telling you that you'll survive, but you cannot work for 18 months. If you cannot work for 18 months, where are you going to get income from? I'll wait for you to think about that answer. Yep, I'm still waiting...

The answer is **disability insurance**. You should already have disability insurance. Again, this stuff is pennies on a dollar. If you get sick or hurt and unable to work, you still need income coming into your household. Your bills do not stop even if you are unable to pay them.

You are your largest asset. Chances are that your earning potential will bring in more income than any investment ever will. Many employers offer some sort of disability coverage. It is usually not 100% of your income.

Remember, your lifestyle depends on you bringing 100% of your income home, so make sure the income doesn't stop if you happen to slip down a flight of stairs and can't work for a period of time. Disability insurance has an elimination period and that is the time you must wait before you can collect disability income. The longer the elimination period, the less expensive the premium will be. I typically encourage a 90-day elimination period because it makes the premium very affordable, and you should be able to get by for three months on your emergency money on the side. You should have at least three months of living expenses set aside for yourself if an emergency arises. We will discuss this more in Chapter 5.

This next type of insurance is probably the most underrated. It can wear many hats. It's the ultimate workhorse, but people don't like talking about it because it's not the glamorous show horse that crowds cheer for. Its primary function is to be used to leave a legacy behind to protect your loved ones, but the money generated can also be used on yourself in the near future.

If I were to tell you that one vehicle can be designed for you with all the features below, what would your guess be?

- tax-free growth
- additional dividends (dividends are when the company has a profit, and they pay a portion of that profit to their policy owners in the form of a dividend)
- provides access to the money if you need it
- some guarantees are built into the vehicle
- no income restrictions, meaning you can put in as much as you want, and the money is protected from creditors putting their hands on it

If you guessed **life insurance,** then you are correct.

These tools operate like Swiss Army knives because they can perform many functions. They can also be very complex, so I would recommend you contact a licensed insurance agent to learn how to design a plan that fits you.

The most inexpensive type of life insurance is called a term policy, but it will not have all the features described above. What was described above is whole life insurance, which is more expensive. Many people want the Rolls-Royce of policies but not everyone can afford it. There are pros and cons for both. At the end, you should always do what is best for your family.

When purchasing a life insurance plan, you are purchasing a promise to pay. You are giving the insurance company money, and they are providing you with a piece of paper that says they promise to pay your beneficiaries money if the policy is still in force at the time of your death.

Now, since you are buying a promise to pay, it might be good to evaluate that promise. If a guy named Leroy were to tell you that he will mail your wife a large check when you die, you would probably review the truth in that statement by looking at his character, credit, and financial situation.

Insurance companies are the same way. If they promise you something, evaluate them to make sure they can deliver on their promise. You wouldn't want your wife forced to hassle the insurance company for money after your death. You would want that company to still be in business down the line. Look at their character, history, and financial strength. Do the credit agencies rate them as A, or AA, or AAA? AAA is the strongest with some credit agencies, and it means that the company has the strongest financial strength.

No one likes to think of themselves dying, so life insurance is usually last on the grocery list.

One day, I was assisting with an estate planning workshop and a pastor's wife was in the crowd. Let's call her Mrs. K. Mrs. K approached me after my presentation and said that she was a first lady, a pastor's wife, and she wanted me to look at their estate.

Now, first ladies generally have nice cars, beautiful houses, and great lifestyles. Mrs. K and her husband were no different—they had a great life. They were doing amazing things in the community, giving back, and people were cheering them on every Sunday.

What struck me as interesting is how the story ended. Mrs. K's husband died suddenly of cancer, without any warning signs, and didn't have any life insurance in place. Now guess what? Mrs. K lost the cars because she couldn't keep up with the car notes. She lost the church because a new pastor was appointed. She lost her home and had to go to live with relatives, and months down the line, she had to file for bankruptcy. This is a pastor's wife we are talking about who is now one step away from being completely homeless! Who has heard of a story like this? There are too many stories like this out there.

That's enough on this topic. What I have learned throughout my career is that the quickest way to clear a room is by saying the words "life insurance" since many people associate those words with death.

There is a popular system going around these days for people who didn't prepare called GoFundMe, a fundraising platform. GoFundMe is not a life insurance policy. There is no excuse for not preparing.

My 2-year-old son has a life insurance policy. It was important to me that he got one directly after he was born. It is not because we think he is going to die soon, but because I want to position him for future success by locking in his insurability at a young age by not risking something in life happening later, causing him to not be able to get insurance later. And because these plans grow cash value by accumulating compounded interest and possible dividends for him. Although he is two years old, I'm sure when he gets older, he would love to have a life insurance policy that builds cash value on a tax-deferred basis for many years and offers the ability to access the cash values by a loan without tax consequences. The cash value built up can also serve as an emergency fund and is not subject to stock market performance.

This last type of protection tool is probably the most unheard of until you really need it, and then it's too late to get it. The best time to get an insurance plan is when you do not currently need it, and usually the most inexpensive time for buying an insurance plan is when you are far from needing it.

For example, the best time to get car insurance is not after you have already had an accident. It can be ideal to purchase it when you are far from needing it because you can lock in your insurability status for later and get the best rates, exactly like I did for my son's life insurance plan.

My mom is the strongest person in the world. She has been battling adversity since birth. She was born in 1951, three years before the Civil Rights movement started. Her mother, my grandmother, had 12 kids, so my mom came from a large family. Survival was the only theme, which can explain why my grandmother had multiple men in her life. My mom never knew her father. They lived in government assistance housing, which is a fancy way of saying the "projects," and faced survival challenges daily.

Despite starting from the bottom, my mom pulled herself up. She was the first in her family to go to college, attending Morgan State

University. She was studying while also maintaining a job, which was almost impossible back then. She eventually met and married my dad.

Together, they moved out of the projects into apartments outside of the city. My dad drove a taxicab, and my mom worked in administration for the psychiatric department of Baltimore city's circuit court. They raised my sister and I and eventually moved out of the apartments, becoming homeowners in the suburbs. They sent my sister and I to private schools so we could get a quality education. How they paid for that, I have no idea, but I'm sure my dad had to frequently visit Tosski.

My sister and I graduated from private college prep high schools, and we both went to college. I went to undergraduate at Howard University and business school at University of Maryland. My sister went to Catholic University for her undergraduate and earned her master's degree from Catholic University. My mom led that entire charge, sacrificing all that she had for my sister and I. We made it.

After struggling for most of her life, my mom developed an illness. She now has a heavy paranoia and has delusions and hallucinations. Paranoia is an unrealistic distrust of others and a feeling of being persecuted. These illnesses resulted from her life's struggles. She has been hospitalized for her psychosis multiple times, but eventually they had to release her after a few weeks because there is no coverage of **long-term care insurance**.

Long-term care covers the things that health care does not. It is a broad set of services for people who need assistance because of a chronic illness or physical or mental disability such as strokes, cancers, dementia, Parkinson's disease, depressive symptoms, hip fractures, heart attacks, etc. It offers personal assistance with activities of daily living (ADL's), either at your home or in professional medical facilities. ADL's are an ordinary task of life that includes eating, bathing, dressing, getting into and out of bed or chairs, and using the toilet.

The average cost per day of long-term care can be as much as $500 a day. That is $14,000 a month! Can you imagine paying that daily cost for years? This is why people buy long-term care insurance, so that risk is offloaded onto insurance companies and you only pay your monthly premiums to keep the plan in force. Support for long-term care falls outside the scope of Medicare, but Medicaid, the federal/state program that provides health insurance for low-income families, is the nation's primary safety net for long-term care financing.

My mom was no longer on government assistance and welfare because she rose above that situation, and any long-term care provided must come from out of pocket. Therefore, she didn't have any coverage, and her options were only to return home from the hospital and try to cope with life by herself with these conditions and without skilled care. I'm sure if my mom would have known about the long-term care insurance and the wedge, she would have prepared herself as she did with all her other life's struggles.

Someone turning age 65 today has almost a 70% chance of needing some type of long-term care service according to longtermcare.gov. Current estimates suggest the demand for long-term care will more than double in the next 30 years because people are living longer.

"Although the likelihood of needing long-term care rises with age, almost as many people who need such care are under age 65 as are above it—5.6 million persons under age 65 (including 0.4

million children) and 6.6 million elderly, in roughly 1995." - Health Affairs research article by Judith Feder, a political scientist.

Those numbers are higher today. I have seen many 55-year-old working-class couples who can't save during those years after the kids finish college because they have to take care of mom and dad and savings start to deplete.

Summary

Net worth is simply how much you own minus how much you owe. It's not how much you make, but it's all about how much you save. Make a list of all the things you own and a list of things you owe. Subtract the things you owe from the things you own, and you will have your current net worth. For example, your home value, 401(k), and checking account balance are all assets, and your mortgage, car loans, and credit cards are all liabilities. Hopefully you have a positive net worth. The keys to building wealth are: protect your income, save, grow your investments, and pass on what is left to your loved ones. Identify three new habits you need to develop right away to get you on track to unlocking the keys to building wealth.

When purchasing a life insurance plan, you are purchasing a promise to pay. You are giving the insurance company money, and they are providing you with a piece of paper that says they promise to pay your beneficiaries money if the policy is still in force at the time of your death. Have your licensed insurance agent review your current insurance plan at least once per year. Make a list of questions you have prior to meeting.

CHAPTER 5:
Investments

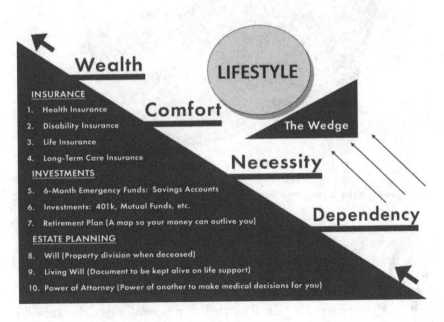

Diagram 1B

The Wedge Folder is the single most significant creation that added wealth to my life!

We just discussed the first four items of the wedge. The diagram displays the wedge holding your lifestyle up, preventing the lifestyle ball from rolling backwards. That is what the first four items do, with insurances. It performs the defensive planning as seen in diagram 1B. Before growth, it can be beneficial if you first protect what you currently have, which is your health, income, your loved ones, and your debt. If not protected, emergency situations can wipe out your finances.

In this chapter, we will discuss the next two items in the wedge: emergency savings and investments.

An emergency fund can help prevent debt increasing from every financial bump in the road, like car repairs, house repairs, etc. It's good to have a liquid fund of at least three to six months of living expenses. Many people lean more toward six months. If you cannot do this ideal amount, then build a smaller one, like one month of living expenses. This could cover many smaller but urgent expenses like copays for insurance claims. It is simply money that you set aside to cover unexpected expenses that could come up.

We will later discuss where to put that money. I have seen it all. Some people put the cash in the freezer, under the mattress, in safes, savings accounts, CDs, etc. Having an emergency fund will provide you with peace of mind, knowing that if something unexpected comes up, you will have that covered. Not having an emergency fund will keep you living on the edge, not knowing if you can make ends meet.

According to Bankrate.com, just 18% of Americans say they could live off their savings for at least six months. That's the lowest percentage of people with an adequate savings cushion in nine years of conducting Bankrate's poll.

It is a sacrifice to build this and it can give you the confidence to handle emergencies more gracefully and efficiently. You will have a higher potential to handle problems like a SWAT team and not have to "rob Peter to pay Paul," meaning not pay someone you owe because you need that money for an emergency crisis that happened. The sooner it's started, the sooner the benefits can begin.

Emergency funds can be a way to protect your savings, because if you are saving for a college education and you have an emergency, you will not need to dip into your college savings to cover the cost. You can use your emergency fund for that to continue building your college savings and not go backwards in your savings.

A common recommendation for how much to put in your emergency money is three to six months, but the most important thing is to simply start. Start with one month and build until you get to three.

Where do you put this money? Do you put it in the freezer, a savings account, under the mattress, etc.? Although putting your money in the freezer could be cool, and perhaps protected from burglars, people lean toward putting emergency money in interest earning accounts that let you access your money quickly if needed. This money is designed to be sitting for a while; it's lazy money. It has no purpose other than to sit until an emergency arises. Since it's sitting, it can be earning interest. Your money is not earning interest while sitting in your freezer or under the mattress.

Savings accounts can be great accounts for saving. The interest earned is not major, but some accounts pay 1% or a little higher. If you have $50,000 saved in a savings account earning 1%, that is $500 extra every year that you will be making on that money if everything says the same. If that money sits for ten years, this is an extra $5,000 of interest earned. How much interest is the money under the mattress earning?

Some people don't trust the bank holding their money because they aren't sure it will be there for them. Money in most banks is insured by the FDIC (Federal Deposit Insurance Corporation). If the bank defaults on returning your money, then the FDIC will cover. FDIC deposit insurance covers the depositors of a failed FDIC insured depository institution, such as banks, dollar-for-dollar, principal plus any interest accrued or due to the depositor, through the date of default, up to at least $250,000. To determine if a bank is FDIC insured, you can ask a bank representative, look for the FDIC sign at your bank, or call the FDIC at 877-275-3342.

It might be best to stay away from higher interest-earning accounts for emergency funds like CDs (Certificates of Deposit) and IRAs (Individual Retirement Accounts) because they have penalties for withdrawing the money early. The purpose of emergency funds is to take money out at any time an emergency arises.

When saving money, a trick I used was to first build my emergency money in another account before starting to save. I did not look at my emergency money as savings. It's simply money that will be spent.

These two accounts were viewed separately. I would build my emergency money first as a prerequisite for the right to be able to save in my other account. I also linked my income-receiving account, such as my checking account directly to my savings account and set up periodic deposits from my checking to my savings account. I didn't want to see my savings for fear of spending it. It was a transfer that happened monthly without me knowing, and it was like my money was disappearing into a black hole that I cannot touch.

A common problem people have is that after saving in an account, they eventually swipe it out, and this cycle continues. It's a cycle of save and swipe out, save and swipe out, become disappointed, and never start saving again. Disappointment is often a lack of not anticipating enough things in advance. So what happens is you roll in with all these high expectations, but you didn't anticipate the difficulties or the challenges that will come up.

The great Jim Collins, author of *Good to Great*, found out leaders tend to anticipate drama, in the sense that they are a little bit paranoid. They aren't paranoid in a negative way, but they are so thoughtful about what could go wrong that they are less disappointed later.

For example, say you are planning to save $500 a month, and you're doing well saving for four months straight. You have $2,000 saved now but didn't anticipate something could go wrong with that money you have saved, such as if your air conditioner unit breaks in the summertime. Now you must take $1,000 of that money saved to buy a new unit. If you don't anticipate those things, then they can really throw you off and rattle you. Then you look at the remaining $1,000 and think to yourself, is that all I have saved? You get discouraged and later spend that too. You try to start saving again, spend it, and then start from the beginning.

For everything in life, if you are going to be financially wealthy, you must take a step back and say, "What is going to trip me up about this?" This is why having an emergency fund is important. For everything I do, I anticipate and say, "What might not go so well?" By anticipating these situations when they come up, I'm calm and confident and not on the edge because I've already planned for it.

It's all about shifting your mindset. For instance, before I start my aggressive savings goals, I create an entry-level task to qualify or a prerequisite as mentioned earlier. Before I can start saving, let me put aside "X" amount of dollars that will be used for emergencies. I have every intention of spending that money when an emergency arises. This is not my savings money; this is simply money that will be spent later when an emergency comes up.

After I have that "X" amount, then I can start my savings in a completely separate account to which I do not have easy access. I put my savings into another bank that is far away, maybe across state lines, and I tell them to remove all of the easy access such as ATM cards, online banking, checks, etc. I do not want to look at this money or access it because I do not want the temptation of spending it. Some banks will let you label accounts, so instead of the generic name of savings account, I labeled my account "sweat equity" just to remind me that it came from hard work. My bankers think that I am crazy, but that is the only way I can protect my money from myself and not spend it.

A popular question when saving is, should I save money or pay off debt first? Saving money and paying off debt are both important to the goal of building wealth. Both require sacrifices.

Generally, it's best to do a blended approach of doing both simultaneously. When understanding the benefits and disadvantages of putting your money toward only debt or only your savings, you will be able to evaluate your own situation better so that you can move closer to your wealth-building goals.

Let's discuss saving first and not paying any debt. If your debt is with credit cards, then you'll pay more money over time with credit card interest charges because it will take you longer to pay them off. Credit card interest rates can be much higher than savings account interest earned, so you would spend more money by paying interest than receiving interest. This debt will continue longer, which could cause you to have debt later or in the sweet years of retirement.

Typically, people do not like to have debt in retirement if possible. You may find that your retirement savings can be cut too much by your debt, causing you to live on a tight budget. Retirement planning will be discussed more in chapter 6.

Having debt can be uncomfortable, but sometimes it could make more sense putting money into your savings first before paying off your debt. If you have debt with very low interest rates, such as during this current time of the coronavirus pandemic in which interest rates are very low on mortgages, it could make more sense to put money into savings first.

When paying debt first and saving last, the drawback is that you won't have anything to make large purchases with other than your emergency savings, which is different than your regular savings, after your debt is paid off. It feels comfortable to not have debt, but you now have limited purchasing power. In the words of Steve Harvey, "You got good credit, but you can't buy anything anyway, so what's the point?" You may have to wait on large purchases, such as a house.

On the other hand, paying debt first before saving could fit if you have high interest rates on credit cards. Paying this down will reduce the dollar amount of interest you pay each month, giving you a larger break financially. There are pros and cons to both, and I recommend speaking with a licensed financial advisor who can help you with these decisions.

Investments are a topic many people love talking about. It is the gorgeous decorating that everyone enjoys speaking about. It can be compared to the feeling of the newly added swimming pool, the landscaping, the custom designs, etc. Before evaluating investments, there are core questions that should be addressed first, such as your financial situation, investment objectives, tax bracket, risk assessment, investment time horizon, experience level in the markets, age, etc.

Investing is the action or process of putting money to work in an attempt to increase its value. Before you do that, it's imperative you consider all of the questions addressed above. When building your investments for your wedge, your investments can drive you fast toward your wealth goals during good economic times, but during difficult economic times, your investments can take you in an opposite direction.

Investing is different from saving. **Saving** can pay a rate of interest that is lower than inflation. Inflation is the price of the gallon of milk that will not be the same today as it will be 10 years from now. So if you want to earn more return than the interest from saving, then you will have to look at investing. Unlike saving, investing is a long-term process. While investing can offer higher returns than saving, it also is riskier. Investments typically go up and down, at least when looked at during the short term. Savings are sometimes guaranteed, but investments are not.

For those who need to grow money quickly, there is something called speculating. **Speculating** is putting your money at risk with the hope that you will get a high return in a short period of time. Speculators can win big, but they can also lose everything. So, the bottom line is, save if you want to protect your money, invest if you want to grow your money, and speculate if you want to gamble your money.

Investments can intimidate people. After this chapter, you will have a better understanding of investments.

We have now moved up from the defensive planning to the offense planning on our needs pyramid in diagram 1A. Since building wealth is our long-term goal, there will be some shorter-term goals that require attention, including major purchases such as a home, or the kid's college fund. If you plan to buy a home in five years, that means you will need all of your money available by year five, so additional guarantees might be appropriate. You might also be risk-averse because you don't have a long time horizon to gain back losses if they were to happen.

Generally speaking, Certificates of Deposit could be a suitable option for this scenario. CDs are a timed deposit and a financial product commonly sold by banks and credit unions. CDs have a specific fixed term and usually a fixed interest rate. The bank expects CDs to be held until maturity, at which time they can be withdrawn and interest paid. A general rule of thumb for investing is the lower the risk, the lower the return, and the higher the risk, the higher the return. Since CDs are protected by the FDIC for up to $250,000, there is little risk, which means the return might be smaller than other investments.

Mutual funds can be great options for beginners to start investing and building wealth. Mutual funds are types of financial accounts that are made up of a pool of money that is collected from many investors to invest in securities like money market instruments, stocks, bonds, and other assets. So, it's like investing in a basket of different securities. It can have lots of diversification. That basket is managed by investment professionals and money managers. They decide what securities to put in the basket accordingly in order to match the fund's objectives stated in its prospectus. A prospectus is a document that provides details about an investment offering to the public.

Remember, investing is the action or process of putting money to work to attempt to increase its value. The money manager's job is to try to organize the securities in the fund in such a way that it can increase in value.

Mutual funds can be great for beginners because it provides investors access to professionally managed portfolios of stocks, bonds, and other securities. The average mutual fund holds over a hundred different securities, which means there is lots of diversification for a low price. It's like not putting all your eggs in one basket.

For example, consider an investor named Buckwheat who buys only Amazon stock before the company has a bad quarter. Buckwheat stands to lose a great deal of value because all his dollars are tied to one company. On the other side of the coin, a different investor named Mary Beth may buy shares of a mutual fund that happens to own some Amazon stock. When Amazon has a bad quarter, Mary Beth will lose significantly less because Amazon is just a small part of the fund's portfolio. Mutual funds can be beneficial individual investments for your wedge.

There is a long list of workplace employer plans that could be a great system for building wealth. A 401(k), 403(b), and 457 are all employer plans that can be a great way to build wealth for beginners. They are retirement vehicles offered by employers.

Many of these plans came about as a response to pensions. The old-fashioned pension was a system that was calculated by the employer that was delivered to employees automatically after they retired. Pensions are considered a **defined-benefit plan**. These days, people also need to save on their own because no single source of income may be enough to ensure a comfortable retirement, so these **defined-contribution** plans were created.

One of the major differences between 401(k), 403(b), and 457 plans is who can contribute. For example, a 457 plan has two types of groups that can contribute. A 457(b) is offered to state and local government employees, and a 457(f) is for top executives in nonprofits. A 403(b) is usually offered to employees of private nonprofits and government workers, and public-school employees. 401(k) plans are offered by for-profit companies. These employer plans can offer significant tax advantages.

Let's take a 401(k), for example. It is one of the most powerful ways an employee can save for retirement. It is the most common employer-sponsored retirement vehicle that enables employees to make contributions that receive special tax considerations, from every paycheck.

First off, the word 401(k) simply means section 401(k) of the US Tax Code that was enacted by Congress in 1978. Many 401(k) company providers offer an employer match, meaning the company will contribute an annual percentage of eligible employees' compensation to their 401(k) account. A popular structure is an employer matches 100% of what you put in, up until 6%, and then they don't match any more contributions after that amount. If you put in 4%, they will put in 4%, and if you put in 6%, they will put in 6%; however, if you put in 8%, they will only put in 6%.

So, let's simplify this for that scenario. Rosco works for a for-profit company called We Sell Stuff To Profit, and they offer a 401(k) plan to its eligible employees, such as Rosco. We Sell Stuff To Profit tells Rosco that they really appreciate him working there so they will put one dollar into Rosco's bucket every time he puts one dollar into his own bucket. Rosco puts one dollar in his bucket and We Sell Stuff To Profit puts one dollar into Rosco's bucket. This process will continue until We Sell Stuff To Profits says, "Alright Rosco, we have given you enough, that is already 6% of your contributions that we matched you dollar-for-dollar in your bucket because we appreciate you. Now if you want to continue putting in more money in your bucket, you can, up until the IRS limits will allow, but we are done for this pay period." Then, Rosco's bucket is dumped into the stock market for possible stock market returns. As illustrated, these plans are great incentives for the employee to save and build wealth.

There is a very special retirement account where you pay taxes on money going into your account, and then all future withdrawals are tax-free, provided certain conditions are satisfied, called a Roth IRA. It was established in 1997 and got its name from William Roth, a former Delaware Senator. IRA means Individual Retirement Account. Some 401(k) plans have a Roth option.

What many people don't realize is when you pull money out of a traditional 401(k) plan, then that money must be taxed. For example, let's say someone is in a 35% tax bracket, and they have a total of $100,000 in their traditional 401(k) at 60 years old and are still working; then $35,000 of that money is owed to the IRS, netting $65,000. If someone has a Roth option on their 401(k), then they can pull the total amount out of their 401(k) without paying taxes because they already paid taxes on the contributions before putting the money in. This can be a significant advantage because there are no taxes paid on the growth after the money enters the bucket.

So, the question is, would you rather pay taxes on the seed or the harvest? There are pros and cons for both. Sometimes paying more taxes can provide other types of benefits with deductions. It's best to contact an accountant or a tax attorney to learn which investment vehicles are advantageous for your situation. Taxes can be a difficult subject to understand because we can be taxed on the same dollar four times: when we earn it (income tax), when we spend it (sales tax), when we will grow it (capital gains tax), and when we die (estate tax).

A Roth option on a 401(k) plan is different than a Roth IRA because there are limits to how much you can contribute and who can contribute. The amount you can contribute changes periodically, but in 2020 the contribution limit is $6,000 a year, unless you are over 50 years old. If you are over 50 years old, then you can contribute up to $7,000. People who earn too much money cannot contribute to a Roth IRA. In 2020, the limit for someone single is $139,000 or under, and for married couples, the limit is $206,000 and under.

Traditional IRA accounts do not have limits of who can contribute, but they have the same limits of how much you can contribute per year. When you pull money out of a traditional IRA account, it will all be taxed, unlike a Roth IRA. Traditional and Roth IRAs are simply terms that determine a tax strategy. You can still invest in the same securities, such as stocks, bonds, mutual funds, money market instruments, etc. Imagine you have a bucket with those securities in it, and your bucket has either a Roth or Traditional IRA wrapper around it for more effect.

Summary

Savings accounts can be great accounts for saving. The interest earned is not major, but some accounts pay 1% or a little higher. A common problem people have is after saving in an account, they eventually swipe it out and this cycle continues. It's a cycle of save and swipe out, save and swipe out, become disappointed, and never start saving again. Has this ever happened to you? Make a list of three things that caused you to empty your savings account and develop a plan to prevent it from happening next time.

Start a savings account in a completely separate account to which you do not have easy access. Maybe choose a bank out of state and have them remove all the easy access such as ATM cards, online banking, checks, etc. This will help reduce your temptation of spending it.

So, the bottom line is, save if you want to protect your money, invest if you want to grow your money, and speculate if you want to gamble your money.

Mutual funds can be great for beginners because it provides investors access to professionally managed portfolios of stocks, bonds, and other securities. The average mutual fund holds over a hundred different securities, which means there is lots of diversification for a low price. It's like not putting all of your eggs in one basket. Meet with your licensed financial advisor to determine your risk tolerance and time horizon so that you can minimize your risk based on when you need to access your investments for income.

CHAPTER 6:
Retirement Planning and Estate Planning

How do you get to the finish line, and how do you pass the baton off to loved ones?

Slowly rising out of bed with no rush, to the sounds of seagulls in the summer, as you prepare your morning routine of drinking hot espresso eating fresh fruits and croissants while sitting on your private balcony that rests on the high hills overlooking the sky blue sea. Savoring your breakfast and enjoying the hilltop views of the sea, you casually open the local paper called *Il Messaggero* (The Messenger) to read about current events going on in your local town.

After breakfast, you leave your house and walk through the neighborhood in the town, passing by the kids playing soccer in the street, the social gatherings in the local cafés, the stylish fashion boutiques on every corner, and the rustic-looking houses blended in with different pastel colors like a box of taffy.

You eventually reach the city center, which is a 15-20-minute walk from your house, just in time to meet your friends at a popular square for the daily market performances. Artists go there to get recognized for their talent in music, comedy, magic, and paintings. You share great excitement, laughs, and interesting conversation with your friends over lunch.

As the city quiets after lunch for siesta, you head to the nearby beach to relax a bit and wait for your spouse to join you, as they were also doing similar activities with their friends. The white sandy beach has water so clear you can see fish swimming in it.

While tanning and relaxing on the beach with your spouse, you look up, and Marco and his wife Alessandra are inviting you and your spouse on their boat for a late afternoon tea. You all cruise around the shore side of the Mediterranean, sipping tea and listening to Marco's playlist of saxophone jazz.

When finished, you leave Marco and Alessandra and return home with your spouse to cook dinner together. Before arriving home, you have to make a quick stop in the taxi to pick up fresh bread from the local corner bakery and some wine from your friend Marino's cantina, where wine is brought there from the vineyards daily.

Dinner is later eaten on your balcony, watching the sunset with your spouse. You enjoy each other's company the rest of the evening, get some sleep, and repeat a different adventure the next day.

This is "Goditi la dolce vita." It is a popular Italian expression that means "Enjoy the sweet life." This life can be very exciting. I know because I lived it in Italy for 10 years before **I ran out of money**. Every day was an adventure. Luckily, I was in my early 30s when I got a taste of this life, and 10 years later received a punishing lesson: without financial preparation, it won't last, and I will be forced to enter the job force again to survive. After that lesson, I can now properly prepare myself for that life I designed.

What about the people who never receive this lesson until late and they are already in their 50s and 60s? Will they have enough time to properly build and save for retirement or will they be forced to work until they die?

I've seen people spend more time planning for a two-week vacation than they spend planning for their retirement! Retirement should be the longest vacation of your life. This chapter will help you prepare for that journey so you can live whatever life you design.

If you take nothing away from this book other than this chapter, then it's still a huge win, and I would be proud to offer this gift. Retirement planning is a game changer. This chapter is designed to be read less as a novel and more as a workbook that motivates you to write an action plan in your personal manifesto about the steps needed to have your money outlive you.

Many people underestimate the amount of time it takes to properly save to have a comfortable retirement. When someone tells me that they want to retire by age 50, I assume they have already been aggressively saving for over 20 years. Experts say that it generally takes an average of at least 20 years to build for retirement. There is a difference between retirement planning and retirement accounts. Retirement accounts were discussed in the last chapter, such as IRAs, 401(k), and 403(b).

Retirement planning is creating a detailed plan of action so that your money can outlive you. It is putting all of your savings and retirement vehicles together on paper to create a map or game plan. The time to have a map is not when you are already in the woods. Retirement planning is so sensitive because you only get one time to plan it right. There is no such thing as a "do over" when you are already in retirement because you no longer have the same time horizon for another accumulation period.

An accumulation period (period of saving) comes before retirement (distribution period – period of withdraws), because when you retire you are no longer working so you will need to pull from your life savings that you accumulated. Imagine climbing Mt. Everest (which is the accumulation and building period) until you reach the top. The top is retirement or the distribution period because now you have to climb back down (take money out). Going down the mountain is completely different than climbing up the mountain because there are different strategies involved. Statically speaking, more people die on the climb coming down Mt. Everest than going up.

This chapter is designed to help prepare you on the climb down from retirement and possibly get you a parachute so you can make it easier and have fun doing it.

People spend more time planning for a vacation than they do for their retirement. I often hear "I am going to always have some form of work because income is always going to come in, so I don't need to worry about it." According to Million Dollar Round Table (MDRT), a 35-year-old has a 50% chance of becoming sick or hurt and unable to work for a 90-day period or longer before the age 65.

Step 1. *Awareness/Plan Early*- Before retiring, you must face the potential of reduced income later in retirement years. You should reevaluate your financial plans now to make sure they fit your future needs. Typically when people are younger, evaluating retirement isn't a priority. It can be nearly impossible to speak to Millennials about retirement planning. By putting a little effort into retirement planning early in life, it can go a long way. Most people are busy raising children and working on their careers, so the retirement planning tin can gets kicked down the road.

Step 2. *Last minute/I should wait to plan*- At the very least, if you don't get to it before, a good time to have a peek at what your retirement future looks like is when it is fast approaching while your kids are in college.

Step 3. *What questions do I ask myself*- **a)** Will there be enough money saved to be successful in retiring, or will working for longer years be necessary? **b)** What about the allocation of your portfolio—do I need to readjust it? **c)** How much will my health care increase as I get older? Here is an important statement that I can't stress enough. **Retirement is never as far off as we believe, so now is the time to get serious about retirement planning.**

Step 4. *Calculate a monthly budget for now and for the future in retirement*- Managing investments shouldn't be a set-it-and-forget-it strategy. Even long-term strategies need to be reviewed once in a while, and some need to be continually reviewed to keep your portfolio afloat. Many people fail to realize in retirement that every day is a Saturday because by not working, they are spending more on entertainment expenses just by increasing their leisure time. It's best to get as specific as possible about calculating how much you need. Managed money works harder, just like anything else that is managed.

People who neither create a monthly budget nor manage their money are surprised to see where it actually goes. Set up a monthly budget for what you think life will be like in retirement when you are no longer working. Categories can include those heavy entertainment expenses such as travel, visiting family, hobbies, and any activities that cost money.

Your overall expenses in retirement typically decrease because many people have their homes paid off and don't have the same financial obligations with their kids. On the other hand, health care cost, travel, and entertainment expenses typically go through the roof in retirement because you have lots of time on your hands. No more driving to work. Let's not forget about food and dining out. During working years, it can be argued more people cook at home than when retired. Who wants to cook at home if every day is Saturday? Make your budget so tight and methodical that you calculate how expensive dining out will be when you retire, and don't forget to add inflation for food cost. Remember that gallon of milk will not cost the same as it does now. (Simply multiply every year times 3% for inflation.)

If you are fortunate enough to pay off the mortgage by retirement, still factor in the other expenses that come along with owning a house, such as maintenance, utilities, taxes, HOA's, insurance, and other smaller costs, like lawn care. Health care, even when you are in good health, still involves higher premiums as you age. Many insurances get more expensive as you age, such as life insurance, and the price of car insurance also increases. This is not something I agree with, but statistically, older people are more of a risk for car accidents, at least to insurers, even if they have a clean driving record. I am typically getting run off the road by Millennials texting and driving, but I guess if I crash, it's my fault.

These may seem like subtle increases but miscalculating the dollars now can lead to spending thousands later.

Step 5. *Make budgeting adjustments now.* You may be wondering why I had you do a budget for the future in retirement when you have no idea what things will cost or look like, but calculating the income needed during your retirement years will allow you to make adjustments to your savings and investments strategies. If the income needed in retirement is low, then you may not need to contribute additional to investments. If that is the case, when getting bonuses or additional money, instead of using that money for retirement savings, you can treat yourself to a new car, vacation, or philanthropy. On the other hand, if your investments and savings aren't large enough to provide your desired income, then it's time to add more money, or create more income streams.

Step 6. *After piling up my nest egg, how do I take it all out, so it lasts a lifetime?* Economics and financial professionals have created something called a safe withdrawal rate (SWR). It is a method that calculates how much a retired person can withdraw annually from their accumulated assets (nest egg) without running out of money prior to death. Depending on who you speak with, a 4% withdrawal rate is what is considered to be appropriate. This all depends on the age you plan to retire so you can determine if that number is high or low.

I'm not going to get too technical here but multiplying your annual expenses by 25 will give you the number you need to have starting from day one in retirement, based on withdrawing 4% a year. For example, if you have a monthly budget of $8,000 per month, plan on accumulating 2.4 million dollars to fund your lifestyle. If you plan on retiring slightly later than normal and working until age 70, it might be justified to withdraw 10% a year.

Next, you remove the emotion from it and try your best to estimate how long you will live based on your current health and analyzing the history of your family's health and longevity. Setting a low withdrawal rate might be a better idea if it's likely that you will live well into your 90s. Nobody wants to run out of money by age 80 and then try to get a job at Walmart late in life. Remember, retirement should be the longest vacation of your life, so we must make sure our overnight bag has enough in it to last us the remainder of our lives.

After retiring, the amount of money that was being allocated toward retirement saving and investing will be removed from your budget. In other words, if you were putting aside 10% of your income into your 401(k), 457, 403(b), or IRA, then that entire expense will be gone, leaving more money for afternoon siestas on the beach with Marco and Alessandra.

Step 7. *Calculate my assistance from Social Security and what age I need to start pulling it.* Social Security can be a huge help, but the Social Security Administration indicates this assistance is not intended to be your only source of funds for retirement. Poor planners arrive at retirement age with not much saved and forced to rely on Social Security. Have you ever seen someone who only has Social

Security checks to rely on, and when that check runs out early in the month, they are frantically awaiting the next one to arrive to give them new life? It's like the dependency a drug addict would have with a drug as they wait on their next fix. It's not a pretty sight seeing your loved ones in this position.

Since you are reading this book, I applaud you for your efforts to improve. As mentioned in chapter 3, you probably won't be one of the people who does not plant anything and then sits back and says, "I hope the government planted some potatoes for later." Figure out your future Social Security income. You can simply go online to get an idea of how much you will be receiving from the government in the future. Go to ssa.gov. Follow the prompts, and it will provide you with estimates of your expected Social Security income at different age points like 62, 67, and 70. It might not seem like a lot to some people, but it does come in handy.

Step 8. *How much do I have to pay Uncle Sam for taxes?* We tend to forget our tax liability, but our most persistent Uncle Sam has a funny way of reminding us. If your entire nest egg is set aside in a traditional IRA or 401(k), once you start pulling that money out in retirement, it will be taxed at ordinary income rates. This will take a huge portion away from your income. If all of your money is in a Roth IRA, then your tax liabilities to your Uncle have been satisfied, and your income will not be decreased. If you haven't done so already, now is a good time to evaluate how your retirement savings are divided up among your different investments for tax purposes. A common theme throughout this book is the word "NOW."

Step 9. *Rebalancing until I get there, just as GPS recalculates as you arrive closer.* As you get closer to retirement, two things become very important in this decade, such as evaluating your risk tolerance, or how you stomach the value of your investments fluctuating up and down like a seesaw, and when do you anticipate taking distributions from your savings. Having panic attacks when the stock market drops can indicate that you might be invested too aggressively, and it might be the proper time to reevaluate your risk tolerance. Consult with your financial advisor because perhaps investing in bonds and other lower risk investments instead of international equities might be more suitable for you.

As you move closer to retirement, you can take small steps along the way to move some assets from riskier investments to more conservative ones. Stay alert for days when the market is rising higher, so you can sell for a higher price. Sometimes it's appropriate to have higher cash balances during times of uncertainty like a coronavirus pandemic, even if inflation can eat away at it. By monitoring your asset allocations, it will make it easier to determine if you are moving in the right direction according to your goals. You didn't hear this from me, but it is okay to watch the GPS every now and then while you are driving. These things can be complicated, so it might just be easier for the professional financiers to handle that part.

Step 10 *Pile up my emergency money, also known as freezer money.* Many research articles indicate numerous people over the age of 50 are not prepared for their golden years of retirement. It's important to increase your cash savings when possible. As discussed earlier, it is best to have three to six months of living expenses on hand. Most people in America aren't able to handle an emergency situation requiring $400 without using their credit. It's sad, but this is what our society has evolved into during the consumption era. As an incentive for Millennials, people who get started investing early on, most of their portfolio consists of the interest that was earned instead of money that was deposited into their accounts.

This is why having a wedge is very important because it builds your financial house in the proper hierarchy of protection, emergency and investments, then distribution of retirement and estate planning. With older investors, it's very difficult to prepare for retirement due to the smaller time horizon of not having as much ability to receive compounding interest.

Step 11. *Consider an HSA.* I had no idea what an HSA was until I was in my 30s, and I only found out then because I read it on someone's Facebook post at the time. The older you get, the more expensive health care costs are, so making use of an HSA can be important. Medical expenses are the largest threat to someone's retirement plan because they will take a significant portion out of the budget.

HSA stands for Health Savings Account, and it is a tax-exempt account you can use to save specifically for medically-related costs. To be eligible, you must be enrolled in a high-deductible health plan. Contributions to HSAs generally aren't subject to federal income tax, and the earnings in the account grow tax-free and the funds can be invested. Typically, the money goes unused for a long period of time, which could help with growth in the market. Some acceptable expenses under this plan would be programs to help stop smoking, purchase new eyeglasses and hearing aids, or modifications done to your home due to medical complications. The contribution limits are different for self-only than combined family, and the maximum amount limits change periodically.

HSAs are attractive because there is no deadline to withdraw funds like in some retirement accounts, such as a 401(k). Retirement accounts have Required Minimum Distributions (RMD). It means if that money hasn't been taxed yet, your favorite Uncle Sam will demand you start paying taxes on that money by the age of 70 and a half. He thinks that you have held onto his money for long enough without paying him, so he forces you to gradually start withdrawing that money, so you can pay him taxes.

The downside to HSAs is if you are under 65 and you decide to use the money to fund a non-medical expense, then that money becomes taxable income, and you could be subject to a 20% penalty. Once you turn 65, the money can be used for anything you want, including travel, but the money will be taxed as ordinary income. It's tax-free if you use it for medical expenses. When turning 65, you avoid the 20% penalty, but you pay income taxes on the distributions that are not used for medical expenses. It will be almost the same as an IRA at that point, but still tax-free for eligible medical, dental, and vision expenses.

Research suggests that the average 65-year-old couple will spend $285,000 on health care throughout their lives. When turning 65, Medicare will be available, but it doesn't cover all medical expenses such as dental, vision, and most long-term care. HSAs can help you prepare for future medical expenses by decreasing your tax liability. Long-term care is included in your wedge for both men and women, but women need it more than men because they statistically live longer.

Step 12. *Estate Planning.* No one likes planning for after-life arrangements, but it is important to think about. Estate planning is the preparation of tasks that are designed to manage someone's asset base in the event they become incapacitated or die. It involves how someone's assets will be preserved or managed after the unthinkable happens. This goes hand-in-hand with life insurance.

If someone dies with debt that they still owe, guess what? Debt doesn't go away. It gets put on to the estate, so if you still have debt when you die, you will be passing on debt to your loved one. It's always better to pass on a legacy and not debt.

Estate planning includes wills, living wills, power of attorneys, trusts, and other tax limit documents. The wedge only covers the essentials such as a will, living will, and durable power of attorney (DPOA) because some other estate planning documents may not be needed at the present moment for people who do not have significant assets. All estate planning is important, but it's best to start and do what you can to at least get a structure in place.

A will is a legal document that expresses a person's desires of how their property (estate) is to be distributed after death. It's like having a remote control that you hold and use from your grave that decides where your things go. It also handles any financial obligations left behind. It's imperative to have a proper will, especially when leaving behind a sizable amount of money and assets. If you don't have much to purchase a will, then it's not a problem because nearly anyone can get a proper will online that is legal and inexpensive. Having a will can make life much smoother for the family that is left behind. I have seen quality wills online for as cheap as $400. More detailed wills can be done with an estate attorney for roughly $1,000, but it all depends on the complexity of your estate. Getting a will now instead of later puts everyone's minds at rest when it comes to handling your estate. We never know when our creator will call us home, but being prepared will make things easier for family during a difficult time of grieving.

Not many people would want their adult children shaming the family and fighting over whatever assets remain after the estate owner's death. This can lead to a lifelong relationship of envy and hatred. With my financial practice and through personal experiences, I have seen family fights at the hospital before the individual has even died.

A living will is another legal document that states the type of medical care an individual who is currently alive wants or does not want in the event they are unable to communicate their wishes; another name for this is advanced directive. A breathing machine is an example of this. Does that individual want artificial nutrition and hydration as a life-sustaining treatment? Again, this is something else that can prevent the family from fighting if this document was in place before the incident happened.

This last estate document is very near and dear to me because I never did it with my mom, and it could have prevented a lot of current mess. A durable power of attorney can be used for both health care and financial supervision of another person. It is another legal document where a person designates someone else to make healthcare decisions for them if he or she is not suitable to make those decisions on their own. A durable power of attorney is often used in the event of a principal's illness or disability. If I were able to have my mom sign this document when she was able to think clearly, I would now be able to get her the medical and financial help she needs.

Her illness controls her thoughts, making her more paranoid of others, and she doesn't believe there is anything wrong with her thinking. To get her to sign a document such as a durable power of attorney now would be impossible, but she would have considered it when she was able to think rationally. She refuses medication that could help her and won't agree to receiving any type of care.

The same thing goes with her finances. If she would have signed this document earlier, it would give me permission to assist with her finances. Now, I have limited control because her debt collectors will not talk to me. I just saw an electricity bill on her kitchen table for $3,000, which tells me this bill has gone months with neglect due to her current condition.

Estate planning was put into the wedge because not having it takes income out of your loved one's pockets. This book is about putting more income into your pockets to build wealth, so we must be careful of the things that can take income away.

With retirement approaching, taking inventory of your financial position for the purpose of good planning and organizing your wedge is critical. With life distractions of raising kids, college, focusing on careers, and taking care of families, it can be easy not to pay attention to taking care of your retirement. Many aren't prepared for the longest vacation of their lives. For some reason, society seems to discourage Millennials and younger people from confronting the reality of retirement planning, but planning ahead is the separator.

Don't be like my client Sarah and spend all your time dancing and having fun without building for tomorrow. Will there be enough money to support my lifestyle later, or will I have to work longer? Will I be able to work longer since a 35-year-old has a 50% chance of becoming sick or hurt and unable to work before the age of 65? Are my investments in line with my goals, and have I been readjusting along the way to my destination like a GPS tracker? How will I handle the increasing cost of health insurance as I get older? All of these steps illustrate the differences between retirement planning and retirement accounts. Retirement years always come faster than we think, so it's time to start planning for it NOW. Retirement planning is the most important planning of your life, so handle it with care. If you need assistance you can call us at **888-7-Retire**.

Summary

As stated earlier in this chapter, going down the mountain is completely different than climbing up the mountain because there are different strategies involved. Make a list of three things you plan to do in the next thirty days to better plan for retirement so that your climb up the mountain is just as successful as your climb down.

Calculate a monthly budget for now and for the future in retirement. Set up a monthly budget for what you think life will be like in your retirement years. Categories can include those heavy entertainment expenses such as travel, visiting family, hobbies, and any activities that cost money. Your overall expenses in retirement typically decrease because many people have their homes paid for. Now, add up your monthly budget for the year. Take that number times 25, and you should get the amount of money needed to be saved by day one of your retirement years.

Make a list of three good attorneys in your area and contact them on what their process and fees are to prepare your will. If you need assistance finding a quality and affordable attorney, then simply send us a quick email, and we will send you a few of our favorite attorneys in your state. Having a will can make life much smoother for the family that is left behind. You can have a will prepared online for as low as $400. More detailed wills can be done with an estate attorney for roughly $1,000, but it all depends on the complexity of your estate. As times change, so does your will. It will need to be updated from time to time as things change.

SECTION 3:
Sustain Success and Don't Go Backwards

CHAPTER 7:
Look Out for All Traps
That Could Take Wealth Away

The first two sections were about helping you obtain wealth, which is possible no matter where your starting point is if you are committed and dedicated to preparing. When most people think about obtaining wealth, it's a vision they believe to be very far away. What typically happens is that it can arrive faster than you anticipate if you're following the appropriate steps. Sometimes it can arrive faster than you can handle. What happens if wealth arrives before you expect it to? How will you prevent from losing it? While wealth is arriving, you have to watch out for all of the traps that could take wealth away.

I'm sure you are aware of one of the most basic rules of keeping wealth is to spend less than you earn. This is a great rule and most people know it, so why do we find ourselves falling into the traps of debt? This book isn't about lottery winners because I am speaking to the people who work hard and honest for their money. I'm addressing the people who build nest eggs and life savings, not gamblers. Seventy percent of lottery winners end up bankrupt in just a few years after receiving a large financial windfall, according to various news organizations.

"Lottery winners are more likely to declare bankruptcy within three to five years than the average American. Evidence shows that most people who make it to the top one percent of income earners usually don't stay at the top for very long."- The Washington Post's Jonnelle Marte

What that statistic states is the goal is not simply to become wealthy but build wealth so that it stays. Even people who start building properly also become victims of the traps of debt. Understanding how debt works will help you maintain wealth, but it can be complicated. Common attitudes toward money management and spending can make it very easy to accumulate debt.

Many people's mentality is to **buy now and pay later**. I was a victim of this myself. I looked at my credit lines and credit cards as my cash in the bank. My credit offered me more purchasing power so that I could buy more. Even when I first moved to Italy, after I spent all of my cash in my account, I had no worries or uneasiness at all because I still had $5,000 on my credit card. I could continue purchasing things as though I had cash. After I had maxed out my credit card, I would pay the minimum balance due on my card and then I had to look for my next opportunity of getting more purchasing power through either cash or credit—it didn't make a difference to me. I would probably be spending more credit because that was easier to get at the time. I paid the minimum balance on my credit cards every month because they gave me a choice. Why would I pay a higher amount of my credit card balance if I could get by with paying the lower amount and fulfill my obligations until next month? I had no clue back then!

What I didn't understand was compounded interest. Minimum payments every month means maximum profits for the credit card companies. For example, after I maxed out my credit card for $5,000, my minimum payment at the end of the month was $150. The credit card company was charging me an interest rate of 19.99%. If I made only the minimum payment every month, it would take me over four years to pay off the balance. At the end of that four years, I would have paid the credit card company an additional $2,357 in interest only, and that is if I didn't use another penny on the credit card while I was paying the minimum payments. That would never happen because directly after I paid my minimum balance, they would put more money on my credit card again after taking their interest payment, and I would later spend that too, maxing out my card again. This process would continue for years until I realized that I could end up paying double of what I borrowed from the credit card companies, and I never even noticed it. Total interest creeps up on you in a sneaky way. At least with Tosski, he charged my dad up front and didn't give him more until the whole loan was paid up.

The credit card companies continued putting credit on my card. That's like handing me the weapon to destroy myself, and I didn't even know it was a weapon. I had a good credit score and my interest rate was 19.99%. What about the people who have bad credit and use credit cards? Their interest rate could be 25% or higher! I now follow my rule of, if I cannot pay off the entire credit card bill in a month, then I will not make that purchase.

According to Forbes article by Nancy L. Anderson, the number one money trap people fall into is **buying things on sale**. People tend to spend money on sales even if it's for an item they didn't need until they saw the sale and then determined the item could be useful. Sales can be one of the largest money wasters, especially if it's not needed.

When you buy something that you aren't going to use, then it's a waste, no matter how much it costs, even if it's only one dollar. Many people buy things from stores only because it was on sale, and they thought they didn't want to miss out on a bargain. This is true not only at physical stores, but also for services, online merchandise, and travel. How many people purchased a gym membership or booked a vacation because it was on sale? You probably weren't going to travel during that time period anyway, but the deal was just too good to be true, so why not travel to a beautiful ski resort when it is summertime and there is no snow?

Nancy's article states a tip to prevent these things from happening. "Ask yourself, would I be this excited about this purchase if it weren't on sale? Meaning, would I normally go to a ski resort in the summertime with no snow? Would I buy this at full retail? Will I use this a lot?" If the answer to those questions is a "yes," then decide to make the purchase.

Another trap is not starting to save now because the **timing is not right**, and you will start later. This is a trap for both people who already have money and for people who don't. For the people who already have money, this trap is typically for those who received money faster than most, such as professional athletes, actors, entertainers, and lottery winners. The money suddenly arrived so quickly, and people think it will keep coming in. The timing is not right to save now because they need that money to support the out-of-control lifestyle they created.

I also hear that trap a lot from the younger demographic who don't have much money. That typically means they do not see the value in taking baby steps now to build because they feel they can make up the time by hitting it big later. They want to do what makes them happy and worry about saving later because it's too much of a sacrifice.

We often tell the younger demographic to follow their dreams because it will lead to greatness. Those constant reminders to follow their dreams can come at the expense of the advice to prudently save, which falls to the wayside because they believe it might interfere with pursuing whatever makes them the happiest. A goal of saving 25% of what they make never received the same excitement as building the next Amazon or smartphone app. Deep down they are holding on to that belief and they don't want to give up that dream because they know how far we have come as a civilization.

I agree, you should always follow your dreams, but you need to also recognize a more practical path, such as a route of saving for things that seem so far away, such as retirement. Don't abandon what makes you happy, but it's a necessity to also make pragmatic choices to set yourself up with a more certain and sustainable path. The fact is if you save more now, you will have more later.

Don't take on too much risk by going after the home run, without first mastering the fundamentals. Save and invest early and often. If people don't save the pennies now, chances are they won't save the thousands later. Money intensifies things. If you are a saver, then adding more money will make you a larger saver. If you are a spender, then adding more money will make you a larger spender.

"I am going to always work because I love my job. I don't need to save for retirement. Retirement means that I will be sitting around all day, and I never want to do that." Sometimes when people feel that they cannot do something, they convince themselves that they didn't want it anyway. Maybe they didn't start saving early and that road seems impossible for them to start at a later stage, so they make excuses why they don't want it.

We learned that health problems are much more likely to increase with age, so a plan of always working is not always practical and controllable. It is a plan of closing your eyes and hoping. Simply closing my eyes and hoping will not bring a book titled *Wealth Building For Beginners* to you, just like your hoping won't bring perpetual health to you. I have to write the book, and you have to exercise and eat properly.

Boredom doesn't have to be an issue in retirement. That is one of the most common misconceptions—people can't fill up their days, which leads to unhappiness. From speaking with my retired clients, if you have planned properly for it, then it can be bursting at the seams with activities and newly discovered passions. A more common problem is finding enough time to accomplish what they want.

If your sincere goal is to work for your entire life, then I don't have a problem with that. Just make sure you are working toward that goal as early as possible with an obsession-like focus on your health and nutrition. If you would like to properly retire, but convince yourself that working is more desirable because a proper retirement seems unattainable, then that is where the problem comes in. **Hanging on to** jobs you enjoy is admirable, but having a ticket to the retirement dance and actively choosing not to go is far greater than not having one at all.

I don't have enough money to save. Saving is a lifestyle. It's a process of paying yourself before you pay others. The amount is less important than the process and habit of routinely paying yourself. Spenders take their paychecks from working and pay everyone else first. After they get their paycheck, they buy Starbucks coffee every morning, making Starbucks' account rich every month. They buy clothes, making Gucci's account rich every month. They pay their cell phone bills, making Verizon's account rich every month. They pay their rent, making their landlord's account rich every month, or their mortgage, making those bank financing companies rich. They travel, making those travel companies rich every month or every year. Then after they finish paying everyone else first, they then try to pay themselves from whatever money is left over from all that spending. That is a classic spender.

A saver does the exact opposite. After they get their paycheck from working, they pay themselves first and everyone else later after only they have paid themselves. They are not reckless with finances because they do a proper budget. They know what everyone else gets, including themselves, before they get their paycheck. They know that Starbucks gets $5 a day. They know that Gucci gets $300 a month. They know that Verizon gets $100 a month. Their landlord gets $2,000 a month, and so on. The point is, they look at themselves as being a bill, just like they pay all the other bills.

The question is, do you pay yourself first, or do you pay yourself last? The amount can be one dollar a month paying yourself in your account because the amount is secondary. After you build the habit of paying your account consistently, the habit will get stronger just like any other habit. Then how you view saving will change and align priorities. You will naturally begin thinking of ways to reduce expenses and earn more so you can save more. "I don't have enough money to save" is a behavior problem, not a money problem.

Some people still don't put money in their 401(k) even when their employer matches. As a general rule of thumb, when your employer offers you free money with minimal strings attached, such as requiring you to contribute a minimum amount into your own account to receive their match, then you should strongly consider this opportunity. Take advantage and make a claim to this money from your employer and say, "Thank you." Below is an illustration of what would happen if you start slowly saving one dollar a year and build momentum by doubling it every year, then you will have over a million dollars saved in 20 years.

The Value of a Dollar

If a dollar doubled every year, what would its value be in 20 years?[1]

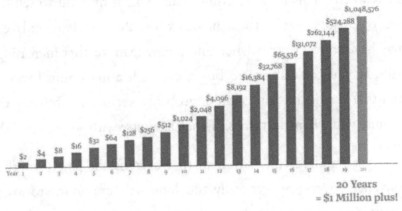

20 Years = $1 Million plus!

Diagram 1C

Long-term auto loans can be a major trap. You have your heart set on buying that beautiful car, but it's out of your price range. The car salesman might offer you a creative solution that you and he will like immediately, which is to extend the loan out to 72 months or 84 months, instead of 48 months. This sounds amazing to you because your monthly payments are much lower, and you can now buy your dream car without worrying if you can make the payments on time. This is also amazing to the salesmen because he gets the commission from the sale.

These days, car shoppers are getting longer loans with many new car buyers getting loans that are 72-84 months long. You will be paying on this car for seven years, which means you will be paying much more cumulative interest. You are also much more likely to have negative equity in the car, which means you will owe more on the car than the car is worth. This negative equity will make it difficult to sell because you owe more than it's worth, and when the vehicle is replaced, you may have to roll your balance into a new loan, further increasing your debt. If you can't afford to buy a car with a maximum five-year (60 months) car loan, you should probably reconsider buying the car because you will make things financially worse with your overall debt.

As a standard rule, any loan that exceeds the length of the car's warranty coverage is generally too long. It's important to avoid the temptation of only considering the monthly payments, and look at the overall total cost of the car.

Have you ever given a store clerk your debit card to make a purchase and was very nervous because you weren't sure the charge would go through? I have seen people holding up lines in the grocery store so they can log on to their online bank account and check if there is enough money in the account to make the purchase.

Banks came up with an idea that will avoid consumer embarrassment and make the bank more money called **overdraft protection**. It lets customers keep using their debit cards to make purchases and ATM withdrawals in exchange for a fee. Let's think about this for a second. So you have run out of money, but the bank is charging you more money that you don't have. Isn't that like kicking someone while they are already down? According to Bankrate, the average overdraft fee was $33.36 in 2019. Imagine not knowing your account is empty, and you keep swiping even for things as small as a $5 coffee. You will end up paying $38 for that coffee. Consumers do not have to choose this option, but most do because not many people want to be embarrassed at the grocery store. Many people who choose this option don't always remember doing so, and they can find themselves still swiping with no money and end up paying lots more quickly in the end.

Some finance experts might argue that if you can't afford it, don't buy it. It might be better to get embarrassed at the grocery store but save more money in your pocket later. Avoid the pile on situation if you can. A Pew Research Center study found that nearly three in four people who overdraft didn't know that they have the right to opt out of this bank service and have transactions declined without a fee if there are insufficient funds in their account.

Putting money into a savings account is fundamental but putting **too much money into a savings account** might not be a good idea. This is a trap because we are always encouraged to put money into a savings account because too many people don't have anything in savings. It's a very responsible thing to do. People who put money into a savings account need to be applauded because they are preparing for their future, but when you put more than your emergency money of six months of living expense in, then you aren't giving your money a chance to grow. By not investing, you could be preventing your money from growing.

Many like the idea of putting everything into savings because it's always available if you need it. After putting in six months of an emergency fund, how often would you come into a situation where you need more than six months of expenses for an emergency available immediately? If your living expenses are $6,000 a month, then that means you have $36,000 in savings. What situation would arrive that would cause you to need more than $36,000 immediately? Since it's unlikely, anything over $36,000 could go into an investment account with potential for growth. By investing the excess cash, you are giving it more potential to grow into a larger sum.

Money in savings accounts generally earns less than 2%. The average annualized total return for the S&P 500 index over the past 90 years is 9.8%, according to CNBC investing. The gap between savings account and investment accounts get even wider over time.

I remember meeting a client who had $300,000 in his savings account, and I told him how much money he could potentially be missing out on by not being invested. He said he didn't like moving his money because he doesn't want to lose any of it, and he felt comfortable having quick access to it within seconds if he needed it. No one can tell you how you must handle your money, but it's important to know if you also share this philosophy, then it comes at an expensive cost, which is the opportunity cost of missing out on potential market gains, in addition to not keeping up with inflation. Inflation is the general increase in prices, like that gallon of milk, and the fall in the purchasing value of money. There is no sure way to protect money from the effects of inflation, but generally, savings accounts are the worst places to put your money long term, because the interest is almost always lower than inflation, resulting in constant losses in a savings account.

The last trap that could take your money away is **being afraid of investing**, which is holding you back from getting started. A survey conducted by Ally Financial reported that "70% of Americans age 18 to 39 know that they will eventually need to be more financially secure, but don't know how to get there. Sixty-one percent of those same respondents said that they found investing in the stock market to be scary or intimidating, with Millennials feeling more intimidated than those in other age groups. And 50% of the respondents knew that they would need to start investing in the stock market at some point, but not right now."

Fear can be keeping people outside of the investment world and potentially holding them back from reaching their goals. Sometimes you have to join us in the pool because the water is great.

I often hear the same excuses from people about why they don't invest, and it's either because they feel they don't have enough money to get started or they don't know enough to feel comfortable. We already resolved the money excuse because in some cases you can get started with one dollar. It's understandable some people are afraid because investments are not guaranteed, and it depends on performance. There is a lot to know about investments, so it might be best to contact a financial professional because there are many investments that can be suitable and match your risk tolerance. I'm sure you have heard that investing is important because it's the best way to grow your money over time.

Summary

Next time you make a purchase of something that is "on sale" ask yourself, would I be this excited about this purchase if it weren't on sale? Will you use this item a lot? If not, you may want to wait on the purchase and see if the desire for it goes away since you may not have needed it in the first place.

If your sincere goal is to work for your entire life, then I don't have a problem with that. Just make sure you are working toward that goal as early as possible with an obsession-like focus on your health and nutrition. Start a morning nutrition routine for 20 days and see if it sticks for 20 plus years. Water is cheaper than Starbucks coffee and keeps you hydrated, unlike coffee. Good hydration equals better health. Research it! Developing some structure in your life will help you build good habits when it comes to planning for your retirement.

Contact your bank and opt-out of overdraft fees. You can also link up a savings account with the same bank to cover you in case your checking account balance falls too low to cover your purchase. This will save you money, and if you get embarrassed if your card declines, it could provide the motivation you need to start your 6-month emergency fund.

CHAPTER 8:
Develop Your Purpose

I n the last chapter, we learned in our own self-protection we sometimes block out the very thing we deserve. When you arrive at the end of your life, what questions will you ask yourself that will determine if your life was lived extraordinarily or not? The questions that I will ask myself are: **Was I authentic? Did I give? Did I have an impact?** Just like building a wedge puts you in alignment with strong finances, action responses to your questions puts you in alignment with your purpose.

Wealth is an abundance of valuable material possessions or resources. Everything has a value. How do you measure your value? Your value can be measured by first defining your purpose, and everything that happens in your life should be congruent with your purpose and who you are.

Notice I didn't say create your purpose, I said define it. My belief is that our purpose has already been created for us by our creator. It is simply our job to define what our purpose is. We are all special and unique. If to live your purpose is the destination or goal, then the questions you ask yourself will be the map that will help you get there.

I often ask people why they want financial wealth, and they can't answer that question. I adopted those questions to be my motto. Authentic for me means, do I consistently express what I think, feel, and need? I noticed the more I would express myself, the better I would feel. I want to feel that liveliness and happiness every day. Sometimes people don't express themselves because of fear of being judged.

I liked to wear Italian suits that are tailored with designer ties and fashionable socks when I returned to live in the US again because it made me feel good. I lived in Italy for ten years, and wearing my suits made me feel confident about myself, because I looked great in them and it gave me an edge. I needed to feel good about myself again after hitting rock bottom in Italy with my finances and my parents' situation. My suits made me feel like I was a part of an achieving society again because I was helping people with their finances to not make the same mistakes I made, and I carried myself highly. You carry yourself differently when you know you are going to be extraordinary.

I remember when I first started doing individual one-on-one client meetings and another senior advisor with another firm said, "Edward, if you want to be successful in this business, you need to take that suit off and put on regular clothes because no one will want to talk to you because you look like a salesman, being so flashy." He also said, "You gotta dress more like me with a basic grey or black off-the-rack suit and tie like the average professional working in finance."

I was discouraged because he was successful in the business, and I looked up to him. I thought maybe I had been in Italy too long, and I should consider blending in so that people will trust me.

Reality was, I wasn't trying to be flashy and stand out with my clothing because I thought I was a snob or better than everyone else. I simply loved Italian-style suits because I felt that this was authentically me. It's my superhero uniform that I put on to save people from financial ruin, and I felt so good in them.

I am happy that I didn't listen and gave myself permission to be authentic because I didn't change my style of dress. Today, I have millions of dollars under my management for clients. I guess people did end up trusting me with my fancy dress because I was authentic and true to myself, and you cannot fake authenticity. The second you start to dilute your secret sauce is when you start losing authenticity. Authenticity was a part of my purpose, so I will never let someone tell me what I can't do.

Sometimes people can unintentionally place their limitations on you because they can't do what you can. I don't think he had any ill will or malice behind it, but it's important that we all walk in our purpose. People connect when you are real. You should be the same in the greenroom as you are on the stage.

In further talks about purpose and authenticity, as I type this chapter, I am sitting in the hospital private delivery room awaiting the birth of my unborn child. My better half is fine and excited as she bounces on the medicine ball with headphones on while trying to naturally induce labor. I am sitting on the couch with my feet up thinking about how grateful I am that we are fortunate enough to set our unborn child up for financial success with their own road map.

As parents, we understand that we have significant influence on how the next generation after us will be set up financially. Don't be silent about these things. Life is only silent if you aren't expressing. Sometimes being silent can mean suffering, unless you are in the reflective, meditative, or spiritual sense.

My next question was **Did I give?** Giving makes us feel happy. Have you ever noticed how great you feel when you give back?

"A 2008 study by Harvard Business School professor Michael Norton and colleagues found that giving money to someone else lifted participants' happiness more than spending it on themselves (despite participants' prediction that spending on themselves would make them happier)."

Scientists believe the dopamine and serotonin released in the brain produces these positive feelings. So, not only is giving back the noble thing to do, but it's also an accepted method to be selfish because you get more positive benefits than the receiver.

Did I have an impact? I want to contribute a gift to the world and future generations. Placing a stamp on the world, beyond my circle of family and friends, will be my special verse left behind. Knowing that I mattered is fulfilling. Once you know what you want your purpose to be, you can start building it. It will influence your day-to-day decisions. Gaining clarity on your purpose can give your life much more meaning. After you have defined your purpose, it will determine how you show up in the world each day.

If you haven't done so already, I encourage you to create your own questions that will be specific with who you are. You also have permission to use mine if they are applicable to your life design. Then, determine how building wealth plays in your design.

Wealth is not only financial. Wealth can also be obtained in diet, health, relationships, and spirituality. Wealth can offer a greater sense of meaning and connection. I have a friend who believes that no one can be wealthy unless they have the 5 F's in balance, which are Family, Friends, Faith, Fitness, and Finances. These things are our emotional tool kit. These things will make you feel emotionally motivated every day if balanced. These motivations can pull you out of bed each morning to be your best.

The loss of any of these things is the first gate to suffering. If you lose one of these things, it makes you not feel like being at your best, and it lowers your desire to continue to be strong in the other areas. For example, if I lose the connection with a meaningful friend, I might not feel so motivated to continue to work out and focus on my fitness. If I lose the love from a family member, I might not feel so motivated to continue building my finances. If I lose significant income, then I might not be so motivated to continue strengthening my faith.

If one of these areas is lacking, then you may not feel as charged to continue strengthening the other areas. When you stop strengthening the other areas, then you will end up feeling unfulfilled and unsettled. If you feel unsettled or unsatisfied, you feel like life is meaningless. Things can go in a downward spiral quickly when your 5 F's are not balanced. These things can help you feel that pull of purpose and make you want to create and contribute to the world.

Let's live our best lives. Learn how to generate the emotion of drive and desire. It's an emotion we feel by having these 5 F's in balance by purposeful conscience design. **My definition of wealth begins with a desire or ambition for more depth, connection, contribution,**

abundance, and love. Only we can decide how much is needed in each of those five areas to declare wealth. For example, in my opinion, Mother Teresa was one of the wealthiest people the world has seen. She had all of the 5 F's including finances. Even today, her estate is worth millions. She saved in the Vatican Bank and raised millions of charitable funds. Her fitness was abundant, and she lived a long life until her death at age 87.

What should you do today to make wealth happen? First, you need to define what that means in the areas of the 5 F's. Remember, all must have a balance in order to sustain. If one of the areas is off, it could make other areas fall off as well.

After you determine what that looks like, the "how" is the least important. Clarity is the fuel that will power you closer. You now have the wedge as a framework with "the how" to improve finances and break the generational curse of financial wealth, and we will discuss other systems to help with the other areas of the 5 F's in the next chapter. Motivation is what gets you started, but habit is what keeps you going.

It's also important to determine why you want wealth. It's easy to say we want it because it can be an abundant way of life, but simply admiring it doesn't produce the burning desire to go get it. I've found attaching that desire with the question of who needs you to have wealth will create the pull toward it. Who needs me to be on my A-game today so I can become wealthy? Sometimes it's easy to deal with our own sloth, but it can be unacceptable for us to have our loved ones go without because of our failure to do things we should do.

For years, I had poor finances. I wanted to change my circumstances, but I didn't have that burning desire to change it. For years, I thought it would be nice if I saved more. Or it would be nice if I had a new house or a new car, or if I had more money in the bank. But those feelings sat idle until I attached my mom and dad's well-being to them.

The moment when my dad was in the hospital to have his foot amputated from diabetes and needed money to take care of Mom while he was in the hospital, changed my life forever. He put aside his pride and asked me for money to help, and I didn't have any money saved up to offer my family assistance. That destroying pain I felt of not being able to help the ones I love pulled me to fix my financial situation so that I will never be that wounded again. You never know how strong you are until being strong is your only choice. I aggressively began saving and building and never stopped since.

Each day, I ask myself who needs me to be financially strong, and it pulls me into action. If it were just me, I would probably be fine with bad credit, heavy debt, and no money saved because I had built a tolerance for it and became acclimated to a lower lifestyle, but there will never be a tolerance for my loved ones being without because of my inaction. It was a mindset change. This chapter is designed to help people unlock that potential. If I don't show up today and do a great job, then my parents and family will have a lower quality of life, which is unacceptable.

God has already sowed a seed of wealth in our hearts; now our creator is simply telling us to water and design that dream. Don't be too casual about your life. No need to be too relaxed. Too much casual means that you are just going through the motions. Gain that mindset shift to go after your purpose.

Summary

When you arrive at the end of your life, what questions will you ask yourself that will determine if your life was lived extraordinarily or not?

Giving money to someone else makes you happier than spending it on yourself. Make a list of areas in your life in which you have made an impact on others. How did you give of yourself or your wealth to improve the lives of others?

Define what your purpose in life is. Be authentic and honest with yourself in your description. If you haven't done so already, I encourage you to create your own questions that will be specific with who you are. Then determine how building wealth plays into your design.

Make a list of three things you could do today to make wealth happen? First, you need to define what that means in the areas of the 5 F's (Family, Friends, Faith, Fitness, and Finances). Remember, all must have a balance in order to sustain. Who needs you to be on your A-game today, so you can become wealthy tomorrow?

CHAPTER 9:
Optimize Your Routines

We often hear that it's our habits that determine outcomes. Part of the reason why many people have poor finances is because they have poor saving and spending habits, and it continues to repeat automatically.

The American Journal of Psychology defines a habit as "from the standpoint of psychology, is a more or less fixed way of thinking, willing, or feeling acquired through previous repetition of a mental experience." So, if our parents have a poor way of thinking about finances that are based on their mental experience and they are influential in teaching their kids how to think, then it can be hard to break this vicious cycle.

In order to change negative behaviors, we must first understand them. Behavior is shaped by a reward-based learning process of positive and negative reinforcement. It first starts with a trigger, then it generates a behavior, and that behavior is followed by a reward.

For example, if I see a nice pair of shoes (trigger), I buy the shoes (behavior), and I feel good wearing them (reward). Each time we do this, we learn to repeat the process and then it becomes a habit. That reward of feeling good wearing the shoes will lead us to do it again.

What if we tapped into this natural rewards-based learning process for saving money? It's like tricking our brains. **It's difficult to save money by forcing yourself to do it on will power and motivation alone if you aren't used to saving.** That method usually results in failure because it's too large of a change. It's best to start building a smaller habit that is en route to the larger goal of becoming a saver. After you complete the tiny behavior that you want to repeat in the future, it's important to celebrate your victory immediately.

For example, when I wanted to become stronger financially by being a better saver, the first step I did was buy an accordion-style paper folder and labeled the tabs to put each section of the wedge in the separate dividers. I celebrated my purchase immediately. The celebration doesn't have to be going out socializing. It can simply be pumping my fist in the air. I learned how significant the celebration part was from a researcher who studies behavior models, behavior grid, motivation waves, domino actions, etc. I never thought I would arrive at saving thousands of dollars a month, but what I did was start very small by buying a generic accordion-style folder, labeled it with the wedge items, and I celebrated by pumping my fist in the air like I scored a touchdown.

Then after I did that, it was easy to buy a $50 safe from Walmart because I already paid $50 for an accordion-style folder, and I celebrated buying the safe with a fist pump. I kept my folder in a safe because it will have confidential papers, which made me feel like I had something very valuable in my safe. I handled my folder exactly like I would handle gold or a million dollars in cash bills.

Then after I purchased the safe, I started stuffing the folder with any statements from the wedge items that I already had, like health insurance and my 401(k) from my employer. I printed the summary pages of my health insurance and 401(k), put it in my wedge folder under the tab titled "health insurance and investments," and returned the folder to the safe and celebrated by fist pumping. Then after I filled a couple of the tabs with statements, I wanted to fill more, so I purchased a small life insurance plan just so I can put the statement in my wedge folder and celebrate.

Then came disability insurance, emergency savings, more investments, and so on. I got to a point where every time I opened my safe to grab my folder, I felt so good as though I was making a major deposit into the bank of Edward R. Williams. Eventually, I completed my wedge, and now I look forward to strengthening it every quarter with newer statements. Long-term behavior change is not complicated, it's just systematic and intentional.

According to experts, long-term behavior change has nothing to do with motivation. Motivation applies to temporary behavior change but not long-term because it wears off. Relying on motivation to change your behavior long term will be a losing strategy. That is where many people fail because they rely only on motivation and willpower to make a big change.

There are only two ways to achieve long-term change. The first way is to change your environment, including your social environment. This is proven to be a reliable method for long-term change, but it's very difficult to do. It could include removing yourself from family members and coworkers. That is not always possible. The second way to achieve long-term change is by making the behavior change small enough. If you start small, it's very easy to repeat and make it a habit.

For example, I want to build financial wealth, so my first step is to buy a folder. I don't need to train myself to become financially wealthy because everyone already knows if you spend less than you earn and grow the surplus that's left over, then you will eventually become financially wealthy. I needed to train myself on making it a habit by making it systematic and automatic. You have to design for the behaviors that lead to the outcome, and do not design for the outcome.

If someone has a goal to become financially wealthy, what generally happens is they start saving and then something happens, and they stop saving and eventually swipe out their money. You must design the plan in a way that makes you not want to regress and go back to how you were. Create many very small habits that will accumulate and get you to your goal. Small habits will all take the route and grow into long-term change, and eventually, all the small habits combined will be hard to undo and regress.

We discussed the two factors to receive long-term behavior changes, now let's discuss the requirements to initiate a change of behavior:

- Some level of motivation
- You must have the ability to do it
- There has to be a trigger or call to action

These are the things that told me to get financially stronger now. When these three things are combined at once together, the behavior change will get activated.

Motivation is needed to start something difficult. Without it, you will never get started. To allow us to do hard things in life is the only use of motivation. If something is not challenging, then you don't need that much motivation. If you can't sustain the motivation for a task that is hard, then motivation drops, and shortly after, you stop doing the difficult task.

For example, I'm so motivated to start saving and so I start. Life happens and I become demotivated and stop saving. Habits are about repeating them. If the disappointment was too great, then you won't repeat the process. That is why it's important to create a system where you will still stay on the course if the motivation is not high, and a system that doesn't need motivation for completion. When tasks are small, they become very easy to complete without motivation.

The only question remains, how to trigger your new behavior to make it happen at a systematic time without you thinking about it. You have to automate it. Research says that if you use an existing behavior in your life and put the new small behavior after it, then you can use the old existing behavior to be the trigger. The trigger is your old existing behaviors in your life, so you don't need to use any other reminders. For example, if I see a nice pair of shoes (old trigger), my new behavior reminds me that building my wedge feels so much better, and I reward myself with a fist pump.

"Plant a tiny seed in the right spot and it will grow without coaxing" - BJ Fogg, author of *The Power of Tiny Habits.*

If obtaining wealth is the goal, access your life and habits, look at what you want to change, break it down into small behaviors, and place the small behaviors in the right spot. The right spot can be after something you are already doing now and allow that habit to strengthen. You won't have to amplify motivation and power.

Other triggers can be time blocks, which is doing a behavior at an automated set time. I have found this to be very helpful because I don't have to think about it. For example, when I set up my life insurance, I chose the date that I wanted the drafts to automatically come out of my checking account. This was my most effective way of saving. I purchased whole life insurance, which grows cash value. Since my existing behavior was to pay bills, this was a method of my paying this bill every month, but the bill was me, as I am building my cash value.

In my opinion, it was more effective than a savings account because the drafts happen automatically without me activating it, and the cash is not as easily accessible as having a bank debit card for swiping out at a nearby machine. When there is cash value in your life insurance account, to access it, you must call either your agent or the issuing company, sign and return a form, and they will mail you a check within seven business days. Also, when putting the money back into your life insurance account, you have to follow the same sequence. There are more steps involved than simply going to an ATM and withdrawing it all. It was a hassle drawing cash out of my life insurance policy, and I loved it.

I have been able to build significant cash value in my life insurance plan because I took an old existing behavior of me purchasing and spending and applied the new behavior of automated saving. Then, I celebrated every time I looked at my cash value on my statements and repeated the process every month. Other time block triggers that work well with building are 401(k)/403(b)/457 plans, and dollar-cost averaging for stock or mutual fund plans.

The money that goes into a 401(k) plan is an investment, which means it's not guaranteed, unlike the guarantees that are in a life insurance plan. During good economic times, investments can grow faster, so it's important to have both guaranteed products (life insurance) and non-guaranteed products (401(k)).

A 401(k) is a great option to save as well since it's triggered by a time block of your pay date and there are strict rules about withdrawing money out. If you make withdrawals from your 401(k) before the age of 59 ½, you generally will need to pay taxes and penalties, making it a great way to leave money untouched. They are a popular choice for investors because they offer a flexible and proven way to save for retirement.

There are caps for how much you can put in. In 2020, the most you can put into a 401(k) is $19,500. If you are age 50 or older, you can contribute an extra $6,500 to your contributions. As discussed in chapter 5, another huge benefit of maximizing the amount you put into your 401(k) is if your employer matches your contributions by any percentage. If you don't put in at least enough to get your full employer match, it's like passing up free money, and as a side note that matching employer money does not count toward your contribution limit. Once you open a 401(k) account, you don't have to worry as much about old behaviors spoiling your savings because most of the time the contributions happen so systematically without you even seeing the money. It can be hard to miss what you don't see. A 401(k) offers great protection against yourself from existing behaviors of spending.

Dollar-cost averaging plans are another way to trigger time block routines to assist with saving. It is a strategy of spreading out your stock or mutual fund purchases, buying at regular intervals and generally in equal amounts. It's powerful because it's a way to set up plan contributions allowing you to buy stock or mutual funds automatically and periodically, such as monthly, without thinking about it. You already committed to buying a regular amount every month or quarter and it doesn't matter when the market is down or up.

For example, if you want to invest one hundred dollars a month into a mutual fund investment, it can be set up so that the money is automatically drawn from your brokerage and invested into your mutual funds account every month without you having to initiate the transaction. And you don't have to see it, just like a 401(k), so it can protect against your existing behaviors of spending money that is very liquid (easily touchable). This strategy is very powerful in a bear market, allowing you to "buy the dips," or purchase stock or mutual funds at low points when most investors are too afraid to buy, which could mean you get the best deals. Dollar-cost averaging helps to avoid mistiming the market, it takes the emotion out of investing, and it promotes long-term thinking. It can save investors from their psychological biases or fear and greed and existing behavior tendencies.

All those wedge items of life insurance, 401(k), and dollar-cost averaging periodic plans helped me with saving tremendously. They all had automatic draft dates for me to pay myself.

Not only did I set time block triggers up for saving and growing money, but I also set them up for managing my wealth with the other 5 F's, such as time with my family, fitness, friends, and faith. I hired a high-performance coach when I first put my foot down and decided that I wanted to get much more out of life. I was no longer interested in simply surviving—I need to thrive! My family counted on me. So, I hired a coach to serve as an accountability partner to avoid drifting back into my old habits.

My coach was instrumental in my success. His philosophy was people, in general, know exactly what they need to do to improve their lives; they simply need to set up systems for accountability and to monitor and measure progress. We monitored and measured all areas of my life that the 5 F's cover—fitness, finance, faith, family, and friendships, so we can improve them. Getting an accountability partner was one of the best things I ever did to drastically improve my situation. My coach's name was Pete Kohlasch. He was harder on me than a drill sergeant and never accepted any of my excuses that I was accustomed to giving to explain poor performance. Pete believes that New Year's resolutions never work because it's a system of setting it once and never revisiting it again until the next New Year comes around.

Goals should always be at the forefront of our thoughts and need to be monitored yearly, quarterly, monthly, weekly, and daily. They can't be a set-it-and-forget-it strategy. After setting your yearly goals, you should break it down into smaller, achievable quarterly goals that if accomplished will lead you into accomplishing your yearly goals. The same goes for quarterly goals, and they should be broken down into smaller, more accomplishable monthly goals that if accomplished will lead you into accomplishing your quarterly goals. The same goes for monthly goals, as they should be broken down into smaller more accomplishable weekly goals that if accomplished will lead you into achieving your monthly goals. The same goes for weekly goals, they should be broken down into smaller more accomplishable daily goals that if accomplished will lead you into accomplishing your weekly goals.

This process is brilliant because it teaches you how to complete daily goals that will help complete your yearly goals, so if you win the day, you will win the year.

In diagram 1D, you will see my daily calculations. I set up a system every night at 9 pm to measure the activities of my day from 0-10 in terms of completing my daily task that will lead to me completing my yearly goals. They cover areas of my life, and then every Sunday at 9 pm, I measure and score my week.

Start building your wealth today. On page 137, there is a blank scorecard so you can enter your daily task for achieving your yearly goals. You must be relentless about measuring your performance every night, and never let a night go by without doing it. After each day, remember the most important step, which is to celebrate your wins. Life is a celebration!

Your Weekly Wealth Scorecard

Date: _____

ACTION	MON	TUES	WED	THURS	FRI	SAT	SUN	TARGET	SCORE	HIT?
SPIN Shake	10	10	10	10	10	0	10	70	50	NO
3 Litters Water	10	10	10	7	10	10	10	70	67	NO
Read Bible	10	10	10	10	10	10	10	70	70	YES
7 hours sleep	10	10	10	10	10	7	10	70	67	NO
Meditate 10 min	10	9	10	10	10	10	10	70	69	NO
10,000 steps	10	10	10	10	10	6	10	70	66	NO
Record Expenses	10	10	10	10	10	10	10	70	70	YES
30 min of russian	10	0	10	10	6	0	10	70	46	NO
Read 20 pages	10	10	10	10	10	10	10	70	70	YES
30 min story time with kids	10	10	10	10	10	10	10	70	70	YES
Nighly Prayer	10	10	10	10	10	10	10	70	70	YES
speak to an old friend for 10 min	10	0	10	10	10	0	10	70	50	No
100 push ups + sit ups	10	10	10	10	10	10	10	70	70	YES

What action needs improvement this week? SPIN Shake, 3 Litters of water, 7 hours of sleep, Meditate for 10 min, 10,000 steps a day, 30 min of learning russian, and speaking to an old friend for 10 min

Diagram 1D

You can download and print this blank wealth calculation on my website at:

www.edwardrwilliams.com/bonus-chapter/.

Your Weekly Wealth Scorecard

Date:_____

ACTION	MON	TUES	WED	THURS	FRI	SAT	SUN	TARGET	SCORE	HIT?

What action needs improvement this week?

Diagram 1E

Summary

If you start small, it's very easy to repeat and make it a habit. Go and buy a cheap accordion-style folder to keep all your statements and wealth-related information in. You may even want to buy a fireproof safe to keep the folder in. It does not stop there; you need to actively add new items on a weekly/monthly basis to build great wealth building habits.

Research says if you use an existing behavior in your life and put the new small behavior after it, then you can use the old existing behavior to be the trigger. For example, if I see a nice pair of shoes (old trigger), my new behavior reminds me that building my wedge feels so much better, and I reward myself with a fist pump. Make a list of three existing behaviors you have that you want to change by introducing a new small behavior after.

Goals should always be at the forefront of our thoughts and need to be monitored yearly, quarterly, monthly, weekly, and daily. They can't be a set-it-and-forget-it strategy. After setting your yearly goals, you should break it down into smaller accomplishable quarterly goals that if accomplished will lead you into accomplishing your yearly goals. Write down your yearly, quarterly, monthly, weekly, and daily goals, and make sure they are easily visible. You can use Post-it notes and write it down in your journal to keep track of your progress.

CHAPTER 10: Epilogue

*W*ealth Building For Beginners is designed for someone who is starting out in the wealth-building process to now have a framework for creating wealth that can last across generations. This is my story of being a common guy with no direction and learning from my mistakes, to build an abundant life and teach others how to do it. As taught throughout this book, "Wealth is not a destination thing, it's a daily thing."

My goal is to be wealthy with my faith, friendships, family, finances, and fitness. What's your wealth plan?

If you start today, you still have time to build wealth regardless of your age. It's not too late, and it's not too early. Design a masterpiece every day. Wealth becomes easier to obtain once the structure has been created.

I am passionate about helping others increase the quality of their lives by building wealth and obtaining financial freedom. People have different reasons for wanting wealth, but generally, people want wealth for either lifestyle and/or leaving behind a legacy.

Lifestyles don't always mean being rich and buying extravagant things. Lifestyle focuses can be on many things, such as climbing up the socio-economic ladder and moving to a nicer part of town, like my parents moving us to the suburbs from a city apartment. Some might want a better car, larger house, or several material symbols of wealth that show you are doing great for yourself.

This book focused more on having fewer symbols of wealth and more on creations of wealth. Not all parts of lifestyle have to include owning a private yacht to cross different oceans. Lifestyle can also be having peace of mind of not having to worry about money and not stressing out paying the bills for you and your family. Lifestyle can mean time off from work to enjoy your family more and never miss one of your kid's school performances or soccer games. Some might want to rent a minivan and travel across the country, visiting each state with your loved ones for a year. It doesn't matter what your financial goals are; the most important thing is you have them clearly identified to move in the correct direction for building wealth and increasing your lifestyle.

Some people may want wealth to pass on a legacy. Legacy is the impact you are having on others. It's the amount of value that is left behind to others. Are you doing good in the world that will leave a standing impression and help others live better lives? Maybe you are trying to be like Mother Teresa and gather a fortune, so you can do good with it by donating it to the poor, opening a non-profit, and making a large impact in the lives of others. You don't need to be rich to leave a lasting legacy. Her legacy still lives strong today after her death. There should be no judgment with anyone who wants wealth for either purpose of lifestyle or legacy. "Rich people aren't evil and poor people aren't holy." There are good and bad people in both categories.

There is a natural evolution of affluent individuals who spend the earlier part of their lives gaining wealth for their lifestyle, then transitioning later to pass on wealth with legacy and philanthropy to others. For example, Bill and Melinda Gates spent the early decades of their life building an empire and now their efforts are almost entirely focused on giving back through their foundation. You can choose your own path.

A large misconception is that you have to choose between doing good and being financially wealthy. Why not focus on building financial wealth and doing good and giving back? The two are not mutually exclusive.

As a kid, I thought having a maintenance man in our apartment complex was a luxury because my other friends didn't have someone they could call on to fix the plumbing right away without receiving a bill.

On the path to finding financial wealth, we must watch out for the three Poisonous P's that could knock us off the path. Perceptions can be implanted into our minds from our parents. It's up to us to make any adjustment to our necessary perceptions. Start small because baby steps count too, as long as you are going forward. Procrastination is a disease that can take your dreams away. Only doing things that are easy and fun won't push the needle forward, just like *The Ant and the Grasshopper*. We procrastinate because we want instant gratification. Too much pride has you comparing yourself to other people and depends on you being better than someone else. It is a mask for shame and insecurity. We shouldn't base our sense of self on a concept in our mind of a set of conditions staying the same because things change.

After you learned how to dodge the 3 Poisonous P's (Perception, Procrastination, Pride), start walking your walk to wealth. Build your wedge that will help you get there. It's a process that starts with insurance. Insurance is a dirty word because it does the roll-your-sleeves-up manual labor and doesn't get the credit for it. It's your protective armor while walking the path so that nothing slows you down or stops you from arriving at the end of the trail where there is a rainbow. You are your biggest investment. Not many investments will deliver as much as you can earn. So, it's important to protect your largest earning potential with disability insurance. Life insurance is the most underrated equipment armor because it can offer protection from harm, and it can offer you significant income while you are living.

Now that you have entered the woods, your investment vehicles will transport you. It's not about how much you earn, it's more about how much you save. I saw a local barber have a higher net worth than a specialized senior doctor by saving more and having fewer expenses. Before you start saving, it could be beneficial to have an emergency fund in a separate account from your savings account. Ideally, an emergency account should have six months of living expenses in it, but if that is unreasonable, start with one month. Take advantage of employer retirement benefits. If your employer matches, then that could be compared to as free money, so grab it. Mutual funds are a basket of different securities that could be great for beginner investors because there is normally lots of diversification that could hedge risk.

The time to have the map is before you enter the woods. Experts say retirement planning can take roughly 20 years to plan effectively. It should be the longest vacation of your life, so spend more time planning it than your two-week vacation to the Caribbean. To make sure your money outlives you, there is a series of calculations that must be reviewed often. It's a different strategy than the accumulation climbing phase of your life. Retirement strategy is about distributing and spending down your assets. More people die coming down Mt. Everest than climbing up. How will we pass on our assets? Estate planning can eliminate lots of family feuding. After all, we want to leave a legacy, not debt. If you haven't already completed an estate plan, then the government will decide where your assets will go. Having an estate plan can be like having a remote control from the grave.

You are on your way to wealth, so watch out for the traps set that could take away all of your progress. Watch out for all the signs that say sales; they could be traps. Watch out for all the people who are freely lending your money and purchasing power like the credit card companies. When you add up all of the interest, you could be paying them double to use their money. Watch out for your alter ego who will tell you that you don't have enough money to start investing. You can start by investing one dollar. One dollar doubled every year, for twenty years, equals over one million dollars!

Why do you want wealth? Who is counting on you to achieve wealth? Are you sure you know what it is? Wealth is more than having financial riches. It's a balance of having the 5 F's in alignment of Faith, Family, Friends, Fitness, and Finances. If one of these life areas is weak, it could affect the other areas. Experts suggest that true happiness comes from having all five in alignment. Sometimes money might be the least significant aspect of wealth. My wealth is that I'm healthy, raising beautiful kids that will become fabulous people, and I'm able to do work that reflects my values. I believe that if you only focus on gaining financial wealth, then you will fall short of happiness because overall wealth is a balance of the 5 F's, and your life will lack purpose by only chasing riches. What are the questions that you will ask yourself at the end of your life that will determine a life well lived?

Create the habits to sustain wealth. Motivation alone is not enough to sustain long-term goals; there must be a system in place that can function without motivation. To achieve that long-term goal, it's best to accomplish a series of shorter goals and celebrate your success. It's been proven that this is sustainable for achieving long-term goals. Automate the system so it can remove the emotions that get in the way of bad behaviors. Automatic deposits with 401(k), life insurance, and dollar-cost averaging could be great ways of automatically building money. Existing behaviors can be used as triggers for the improved behavior.

Wealth building is a process, and our team is committed to constantly providing you the tools to achieve it. Change is necessary to achieve wealth. Either you are going to pick the time and change is going to happen, or change and time are going to pick you as it did with my dad and his diabetes. Stay connected to us via edwardrwilliams.com. Bonus chapters and additional tools will be posted on our website, accessible only to those who registered. We are looking forward to building "Your Wealth Plan" because **Life is a Celebration**.

Summary

Make a top ten list of accomplishments you want to celebrate, from least important to most important, regarding your journey to more wealth. Make it clear what you want to achieve and what would be your way of celebrating, so you have something to look forward to.

Now that you have read this book, take advantage of a free bonus chapter on how to stay organized and on task with your wealth plan. To gain access to the bonus chapter, visit my website at www.edwardrwilliams.com/bonus-chapter/. You can also download the goal worksheets in the resource guide.

"Congratulations! Because you are taking your first steps toward expanding your wealth by purchasing and reading my book, I will gift you a complimentary consultation with my team of licensed professionals and provide you with our Wealth Starter Kit. Wedge™ folder included! Go to https://edwardrwilliams.com/wealth-kit/ to receive my gift. Let's build your wealth!" – Edward.

This powerful book could forever alter the course of someone's life, and it could be you who gives it to them. Your gift helps someone have hope that they can also achieve the retirement they desire.

Write down five people you would like to give a copy of this book to:

1._____

2._____

3._____

4._____

5._____

Thank you for taking the time to read and share my book.

To YOUR successful wealth journey!

Edward R. Williams

Edward R. Williams

Resource Guide:

WilliamsFinancialGroup.org – *This is the best website in the world! The company was founded by "yours truly." We work hard to make sure our website is always updated with resources to assist with your retirement and financial planning needs. We believe everyone deserves the retirement of their dreams, so we built a company around that foundation. WilliamsFinancialGroup.org is the home of The Wedge™ for driving you toward your wealth goals. Our team is ready to assist, so start building your wealth today. Call us at 888-7-Retire.*

SSA.gov – *This site is important for your financial future. There is a calculator on this site that will estimate your retirement income from social security. Follow the prompts and enter your information, and it will list projected income at age 62, 67, and 70. It's not wise to only rely on Social Security income in retirement, but it helps to know how much could be received. It also includes unemployment insurance, old-age assistance, aid to dependent children, and grants to the states to provide various forms of medical care.*

FDIC.gov – *Learn about this independent agency that insures money placed into select banks. It was created by the US Congress to maintain stability and public confidence in the* nation's financial system. The goal of the FDIC is to insure deposits and examine and supervise financial institutions for safety and soundness for consumer protection. It was created in 1933 in response to the thousands of bank failures that occurred in the 1920s and early 1930s. Check here to learn if your bank is FDIC insured.

Longtermcare.acl.gov – This is a resource for learning about long-term care and how to qualify. This website helps you take an active role in planning for your potential long-term care needs. It provides in-depth and objective information about the risks and costs of long-term care, the importance of planning, and the public and private planning and financing options that are available. There is also a free planning guide that can be ordered by mail or downloaded from the site.

Medicare.gov – This is the official federal government website for Medicare. Medicare is the country's health insurance program for people aged 65 or older. When you have Medicare and other types of coverage, Medicare works with your other insurance to coordinate who pays first. The primary payer is the insurance that pays for your medical bills first, up to the coverage limits, and then sends the remaining balance to the secondary payer. Learn how it works.

Bankrate.com – *Provides free rate information to consumers on more than 300 financial products for mortgages, credit cards, car loans, CDs, money market accounts, ATM fees, home equity loans, and online banking fees. This is a great company to view comparisons; however, you should do your due diligence and research the legitimacy of the lenders. A bank rate is the interest rate at which a nation's central bank lends money to domestic banks, often in the form of very short-term loans. This site also has calculators for calculating the total interest rate, measured in dollars, paid from credit cards.*

USA.gov – *This is the official government site for learning how to create an estate plan. A good estate plan can give the maximum allowed by law to your beneficiaries and the minimum to the government. This website can be a great resource for learning the rules. A written will is a practical first step in estate planning. If you do not have a will when you die, your estate will be handled in probate court. Your property could be distributed differently from what you would like. There is also information on establishing power of attorneys and trusts.*

3 Month Vision Worksheet
How I'd like my life to be

INSTRUCTIONS: Allow yourself 20 minutes of quiet time to consider these questions that help you create and shape your vision for your next 3 months. Write your answers in the PRESENT tense, and be as SPECIFIC as you can.

1. How do I want my life to be? Write below how you'd like each area to be in 3 months' time:

i) Personal Life, Home and Family

ii) Career, Work and Business Life

iii) Health and Well-being

iv) Finances and Wealth Building

v) Community, Friendships

vi) Spiritual and Learning

vii) Write anything else, that you perhaps haven't mentioned yet here:

2. What if there were no obstacles?

3. Who do you need to BE to achieve this? I need to be someone who is

4. If there was one important CHANGE you could make over the next 3 months, what would it be?

5. My THEME for the next 3 months is: _____

Wacky Wild Wealth Goal Brainstorming

INSTRUCTIONS: Everyone says how important it is to have goals, but sometimes we don't know where to start. The purpose of this exercise is to **brainstorm** potential goals and **identify up 10 possible areas that could be turned into goals.** You can do all 5 stages in one sitting, but it works well to allow yourself 1-2 weeks to complete all the steps - including returning to your initial brainstorm to add anything you may think of afterwards!

1. FIRST, BRAINSTORM a Wacky, Wild List of everything you want in your lifetime!
   - List below all the **Wacky, Wild** (and normal!) **things** you want to **BE, DO and HAVE** in life!
   - Aim for **at least 50 items** from big to small, ANYthing and EVERYthing you can think of.
   - **Write as quickly as you can,** keeping your **answers brief** and **on one page.** This is a brainstorming exercise, so nothing is ruled out. **Everything should be included** from the mundane to the extreme.
   - As this is a 'stream of consciousness' approach, **duplicates, silly and meaningless answers are just fine.**

Wacky Wild Wealth Goal Brainstorming

2. **DISCOVER WHICH GOALS are most meaningful for you:** Now, beside each item on your Wacky Wild Wealth Goal Brainstorm List on page 1, give it a score of 1 for EACH element on the 'Wheel of Life' that would be improved should you achieve that goal. The maximum possible score for any item on your brainstorming list is therefore 8.

EXAMPLE:

If you had "Own a Ferrari" as one of your goals, would it improve your 1) Career? 2) Money? 3) Health? 4) Friends and Family? 5) Significant Other/Partner? etc. Perhaps it would **score a total of 1** on your wheel (Fun).

And if you had "Get a Dog" as a goal, would it improve your 1) Career? 2) Money? 3) Health? 4) Friends and Family? 5) Significant Other/Partner? etc. Perhaps this goal would **score a total of 4** on your wheel (Health, Personal Growth, Fun, Home).

The elements/headings from the Wheel of Life are:

1. Career
2. Money/Wealth
3. Health
4. Friends and Family
5. Significant Other/Partner
6. Personal Growth and Learning
7. Fun, Leisure and Recreation
8. Physical Environment/Home

Note: Be honest – only give it a point if it TRULY improves an element on your wheel. And yes, you can score ½ points!

3. **REVIEW YOUR LEARNINGS.** Take another look at your Wacky Wild Wealth Goal Brainstorm List on page 1:

Which goals have the highest scores? _____

_____

Which goals have the lowest scores? _____

_____

What surprises (if any) are there as you review your scores? _____

_____

_____

Where do you normally place your focus in life? Why do you think that is? _____

_____

_____

What have you learned about yourself so far from this exercise? What common themes are there? What else?

_____

_____

_____

Wacky Wild Wealth Goal Brainstorming

4. **SELECT 10 items from your list as possible goals.** These don't have to be your highest scoring items, but they probably will have high scores. And now in one brief sentence write below WHY the goal is important to you.

   IMPORTANT NOTE: If you are unable to come up with a good justification – ask yourself why is it still on the list?

1. _____ is important to me because _____
   _____

2. _____ is important to me because _____
   _____

3. _____ is important to me because _____
   _____

4. _____ is important to me because _____
   _____

5. _____ is important to me because _____
   _____

6. _____ is important to me because _____
   _____

7. _____ is important to me because _____
   _____

8. _____ is important to me because _____
   _____

9. _____ is important to me because _____
   _____

10. _____ is important to me because _____
    _____

So, you now have 10 possible goals to work with. Finally, just before we wrap up this exercise, ponder:

5. What are the key learnings that you'd like to make a note of and take away?

1st Key Observation/Learning _____

2nd Key Observation/Learning _____

3rd Key Observation/Learning _____

BACKGROUND
- We live busy lives and for many of us, finding time to ponder and reflect on what we want from life seems a waste of our precious time - or simply a distraction from the other 101 things we have on our lists.
- But if you're not clear on what you want it's impossible to have direction - we end up going wherever life takes us. We could end up anywhere or everywhere.
- Not knowing what we want also makes it hard to say "No" to others. How can we prioritise ourselves when we have nothing to work towards for ourselves? We have no REASON to say no.
- Having goals also gives us purpose in life. When we KNOW what we want, we can get focused and ask ourselves, "Does this move me towards my goals - or away from?"
- "If you don't know what you want, you'll end up with what you get!" So, let's get started.

INSTRUCTIONS
1) Create a space in your busy schedule.
2) Find a quiet spot - or a nice cosy coffee shop where you won't be interrupted by your normal life.
3) Answer the questions below!

 Part 1 - Brainstorming Ideas

The purpose of this exercise is to brainstorm goal ideas and identify 5 ideas that could be turned into goals.

i.   So, with each of the 2 lists below, aim for **as many items as you CAN** from big to small - ANYthing and EVERYthing you can think of.
ii. Then CIRCLE 5 of your ideas as possible goals - the first 5 things that grab you, get you inspired or excited.

1. List below all the **things** you want to **BE, DO and HAVE** in the next 1-5 years:

2. List below everything you **DON'T WANT** to **BE, DO and HAVE** in the next 1-5 years:

**Annual
Goal Setting Worksheet**

 ### Part 2 - Refining your Ideas

Working towards unexciting goals is a hard slog. So we're just checking your 5 potential goals and making sure they're exciting for you before you go any further.

Write the Top 5 items you MAY like to work with: Pick 5 things you might like to work on for the coming year. You can use the 5 ideas from Part 1 or anything else you can think of that you may want to work on in the year ahead.	What would achieving this goal do for YOU? How will you FEEL, How will your life be different?	How EXCITING is this goal? Score it out of 10 below
1.		_____ / 10
2.		_____ / 10
3.		_____ / 10
4.		_____ / 10
5.		_____ / 10

Are you Excited? If your Excitement Score is 8 or more – Congratulations, you have found great goals! But if your Excitement Score is less than 8, you may want to reflect on what would make that goal's score higher before continuing with it.

 ### Part 3 - Set Your Goals!

Now it's time to pick 3 goals to actually work with. The best goals are:

a) **Aligned with your values.** The more a goal aligns with your inner or core values – the EASIER it will be to achieve. (NB. You can achieve goals that don't align with your values but it's usually harder and less satisfying.) Trust your gut instinct here.
b) **Stated in the positive.** Focus on what you WANT ie. "I want healthy fingernails" rather than "I want to stop biting my nails." This gives you a clear visual to work towards rather than a constant reminder of what you don't want.
c) **SPECIFIC!** The more specific you are, the easier it is to keep steering in the right direction - and the easier it is to achieve!

Write below the 3 Goals you WILL actually work with: Review what you've done so far and choose 3 goals for yourself. What would you be disappointed if you DIDN'T achieve?	Why bother? What outcome are you looking for? WHY do you want this goal? What are the BENEFITS to you?	WHEN will you achieve it by? A date to aim for & inspire you, not beat yourself up with	HOW will you know you've achieved your goal? What and how can you prove it has been completed?
1. _____	• • •	Month Year _____ / 2____	
2. _____	• • •	Month Year _____ / 2____	
3. _____	• • •	Month Year _____ / 2____	

Excellent! Now let's take a look at how you can help yourself achieve these and how you might get in your own way.

Annual
Goal Setting Worksheet

Part 4 - Preparing for Success

i. Success Accelerators:	**ii. Smash those Obstacles:**	**iii. What is the best advice I could give myself to make sure I achieve these goals?**
What can I start doing, stop doing, do more or less of that will help me achieve my goals?	What could get in the way? If you were going to sabotage yourself how would you do it?	
_____	_____	_____
_____	_____	_____
_____	_____	_____

Part 5 - Taking Action

So, what ONE thing will you do for EACH goal in the next month? (Yes, you can start now!)

Write out ONE action you will complete towards EACH goal in the NEXT MONTH. This is the FIRST STEP. Break the action down into a smaller step or action until you can commit 100%. If you want to do more than one action, great, but there must be a minimum of ONE.

GOAL 1 Action _____ by _____

GOAL 2 Action _____ by _____

GOAL 3 Action _____ by _____

And finally, what ONE action will I start tomorrow? _____

Part 6 - Support and Commitment

WHO will help & support me? Who are my CHEERLEADING TEAM?
Eg. Your personal trainer, coach, a friend, gym-partner, family, a work colleague. Get specific as to how they can support you.

1. Who _____ HOW Specifically? _____

2. Who _____ HOW Specifically? _____

3. Who _____ HOW Specifically? _____

Who will you have to BE to achieve these goals? _____

❏ **I am committed to achieving my goals**   **Signed** _____

Congratulations! Just one more step. To really COMMIT to your goals, complete the Goal Summary Sheet on the next page.

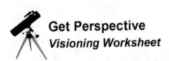

Get Perspective
Visioning Worksheet

1. **What is your ultimate wealth building goal? Do you want to retire early? Do you have a plan as to what your life would be like in retirement?**

2. **What if there were no obstacles?**

3. **What do you want to be doing (career and personal life):**

   i) 10 years from now

   ii) 5 years from now

   iii) 2 years from now

   iv) 1 year from now

   v) 6 months from now

   vi) 3 months from now

Goals Motivator
Find Your Hidden Treasure!

Why we want our goals is totally unique to us. A pay-rise may mean self-esteem and validation, or it could mean security, a holiday or getting married. Once we understand WHY we want our goals, and why we want our goals NOW, it's easier to focus, go the "extra mile" and find that extra energy to put into our goals.

To get the most out of this exercise, I want you to be *totally honest* with yourself and lose the self-judgement. Write whatever pops into your head - however silly or boring it might seem.

> **Write Your Biggest Wealth Goal Here:**

1. First, score out of 10, how motivated you are currently to achieve this goal: _____ / 10

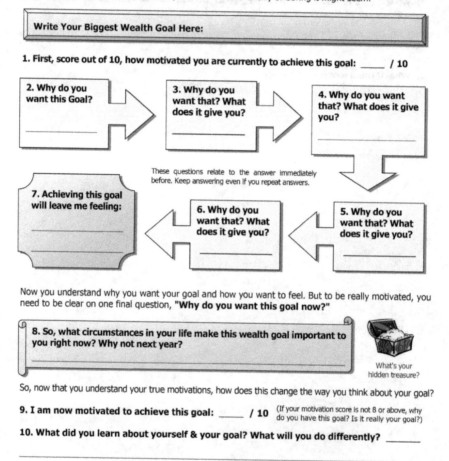

2. Why do you want this Goal?

3. Why do you want that? What does it give you?

4. Why do you want that? What does it give you?

These questions relate to the answer immediately before. Keep answering even if you repeat answers.

7. Achieving this goal will leave me feeling:

6. Why do you want that? What does it give you?

5. Why do you want that? What does it give you?

Now you understand why you want your goal and how you want to feel. But to be really motivated, you need to be clear on one final question, **"Why do you want this goal now?"**

> **8. So, what circumstances in your life make this wealth goal important to you right now? Why not next year?**

What's your hidden treasure?

So, now that you understand your true motivations, how does this change the way you think about your goal?

9. I am now motivated to achieve this goal: _____ / 10   (If your motivation score is not 8 or above, why do you have this goal? Is it really your goal?)

10. What did you learn about yourself & your goal? What will you do differently? _____

NAIL that Goal!
SMART Wealth Goal-Setting

Name _____   **Date** _____ Day   Month   Year

Write Your SMART Wealth Goal Here _____
(Pick one goal to work with. Then see next page for description of SMART and help with writing successful goals)

_____ **by** ___ Day   Month   Year

Motivation	
WHY I want this goal (the 'outcome/s' you are looking for)	
List ALL the Benefits here (of achieving your goal)	
The BIG Benefit (of achieving goal)	
What is the PAIN? (of not achieving your goal)	
Achieving this Goal will also help me (other areas)	
Obstacles (also known as your secondary gain)	
I need to be aware that the BENEFIT to me of NOT completing my goals is	Note: It's ESSENTIAL that you have some answers in this box
Other obstacles to my success include	
Set Goal Levels (eg. your goal could vary on time, quantity, quality)	
MINIMUM	
TARGET	
EXTRAordinary	
How will you need to BE different? (a worthwhile goal often requires us to look at / do things differently)	
In order to achieve this goal I will START doing	
In order to achieve this goal I will STOP doing	
In order to achieve this goal I will need to BE someone who is	
Moving Forwards (eg. things, people, personal qualities, information, knowledge, skills, finance etc.)	
Resources available	
Resources I will need	
Taking ACTION (make these things EASILY achievable so you feel good about taking action!)	
3 steps I will complete in the next WEEK that move me closer to my goals	1. 2. 3.
3 steps I can complete in the next MONTH that move me closer to my goals	1. by 2. by 3. by

NAIL that Goal!
SMART Wealth Goal-Setting

ALL ABOUT SMART WEALTH GOALS - They are:

1) Stated in the POSITIVE. We tend to get what we focus on. Whenever we say "I want to stop biting my fingernails" our brain has to first build a picture of what you DON'T want – bitten fingernails - in order not to do it. Try NOT thinking of an alligator biting your toe...
> EXAMPLES
> *Eg. "I have healthy fingernails" rather than "I want to stop biting my nails"*
> *Eg. "I weigh 150lbs" rather than "I want to lose 20lbs"*

2) Stated in the PRESENT TENSE. This helps the brain to assume you will be successful!
> EXAMPLES
> *Eg. On 30th September I have healthy fingernails/have a new job/am running a mile in 8 minutes*

3) Use the Acronym "SMART"

- **S**pecific (the more specific you are the easier your goal is to achieve)
- **M**easurable (so you know when you have achieved it)
- **A**ction-oriented (ie. you can DO something about it! Is it within your control? ie. Winning the lottery is not a "SMART" goal)
- **R**ealistic (Goals need to be both challenging to inspire you AND realistic so you set yourself up for success)
- **T**ime-Bound (has a deadline)

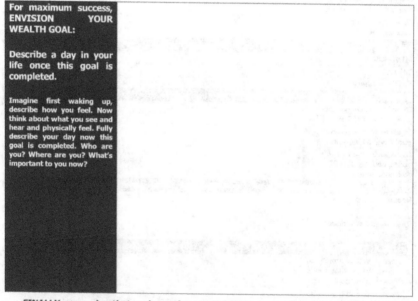

For maximum success, ENVISION YOUR WEALTH GOAL:

Describe a day in your life once this goal is completed.

Imagine first waking up, describe how you feel. Now think about what you see and hear and physically feel. Fully describe your day now this goal is completed. Who are you? Where are you? What's important to you now?

FINALLY, remember that goals are there to INSPIRE you, not to beat yourself up with!

Life Visioning Exercises

"Rocking Chair" Life Vision

INSTRUCTIONS:
- Do you ever wonder what your life dream is? This exercise helps you see the vision you *already have within you* for your life.
- Allow yourself 20 minutes of quiet time to ponder and write your answer in the space below!
- This is about YOU, so let your imagination go, **write a story and paint a picture of your life with words.**

Now, take a moment to REALLY imagine you are blissfully happy and healthy AND 90 years old. You're **sitting in your rocking chair** and looking back over your **IDEAL life**.

1. **Who are you** as a person? What is it about you that **people value**?
2. What have you **achieved?** What are you **proud of**? What added meaning to your life and gives you a sense of **fulfillment**?
3. Perhaps consider how your life unfolded in the following areas; **Family**, **Friends**, **Significant Other**, **Wealth**, **Career**, **Health** (emotional, spiritual and physical), your **Home**, what you did for **Fun and Leisure**, what you **Learned** about, what you did in **Service**, **Leadership** or in your **Community**.
4. Finally I wonder what you can **see** around you? What are you **feeling**? What can you **hear**? What SHOWS you're truly happy?

Tip: The complete picture may not magically arrive, just put pen to paper NOW and write – see what happens!

Life Visioning Exercises

Retirement - or Big Birthday - Party Visioning Exercise

BACKGROUND:

- This visioning exercise involves you imagining some point in the future when you're going to retire. If you don't work (or can't imagine retiring) it could also be a "Big" Birthday party, perhaps your 60th, 65th or 70th Birthday.
- This party has been organized to celebrate you and a substantial change you're making in your life. Are you retiring - or maybe you're moving somewhere new? Perhaps you're going travelling or embarking on a new creative career? Only you know!
- However you got here, a big party is being held in your honour. This party is celebrating YOU.

So, take a moment to imagine that you're at a party all about you! Someone has written a speech celebrating you. What would it say? Use the question prompts below to help you write the speech that someone will read ABOUT you in the space below.

1. How old are you? Who is at the party? Where is the party being held?
2. What have you achieved in your family, career, wealth, business, community or in the world?
3. What is it about you that the **people at the party truly value**?
4. What would YOU want to be said about you? What would you be disappointed if it was not said?
5. What did you do that was truly amazing? Where did you surprise yourself? Where did you surprise others? What are you MOST proud of? What mistakes did you make, that you can laugh about now?
6. What is the essence of you that you would want to be captured in that retirement or birthday speech?
7. **Optional:** Where are you going next in your life? What are you excited to spend more time doing? How do your friends and family fit into your life going forwards?

Final Tip: Don't worry about writing a "good speech" - instead concentrate on what the speaker might say - if it helps, imagine this is a first draft of the speech, just to capture the key points. And remember to write the speech in the 3rd person eg. "Sarah/Auntie Sarah has always...":

"Life is a Celebration!" Edward R. Williams

Life Visioning Exercises

"Newspaper Article" Writing Exercise

BACKGROUND:
- This visioning exercise involves you imagining you have achieved a great milestone in your life or career.
- What would success look like for you?
- It could be an award you've received, a book you've written, something you've established or created. It could be a fund-raising goal you reached, a feat of travel, charitable activities or something else.
- Now, write an article as if written by a newspaper about the recent milestone and successes you have achieved.

Tips

1. Write from 250-500 words in in the PAST tense.
2. Mention yourself, anyone who helped you and any sources quoted - by name.
3. Remember to give a little background including recent successes and other relevant highlights.
4. What does your success MEAN for the people reading it - how do the readers benefit?
5. OPTIONAL: What newspaper would you like to be featured in? Try (as best you can) to write in that newspaper's style.

Final Tip: Don't worry about grammar or spelling here - this is about capturing your vision and essence.

Understanding Our Wealth Goals
The "Why" of Wealth Goals

Whether we achieve our goals depends on whether we take action. But what decides whether we take action in the first place? How motivated you are! So, simply **pick your Top 3 wealth goals**, then **answer the questions below**. Keep writing even if you repeat your answers. The information below will help you feel clear, focused and more motivated to achieve your goals.

Write Wealth Goal No. 1 Here:	**Write Wealth Goal No. 2 Here:**	**Write Wealth Goal No. 3 Here:**
Why do you want this Goal? What does it give you?	**Why do you want this Goal? What does it give you?**	**Why do you want this Goal? What does it give you?**
And why do you want that? What does that give you?	**And why do you want that? What does that give you?**	**And why do you want that? What does that give you?**
And why do you want that? What does that give you?	**And why do you want that? What does that give you?**	**And why do you want that? What does that give you?**
And why do you want that? What does that give you?	**And why do you want that? What does that give you?**	**And why do you want that? What does that give you?**
What will this goal help you feel?	**What will this goal help you feel?**	**What will this goal help you feel?**